Hidden Gems

Dennis C. Williams, Jr.

CROSSBOOKS'
PUBLISHING

CrossBooks™
A Division of LifeWay
1663 Liberty Drive
Bloomington, IN 47403
www.crossbooks.com
Phone: 1-866-879-0502

First published by CrossBooks 9/23/2011

ISBN: 978-1-4627-0617-4 (sc)
ISBN: 978-1-4627-0618-1 (hc)
ISBN: 978-1-4627-1096-6 (e)
Library of Congress Control Number: 2011915814

Printed in the United States of America

This book is printed on acid-free paper.

Table of Contents

Acknowledgements

It was thirteen years ago that my friend Rusty challenged me to pray for transformation in the church. He believed in the power of intercessory prayer. I didn't; it seemed to violate people's freedom of choice. Both of us were frustrated with the tepid attitude of our church. I was determined to see what the Bible had to say on the subject. Reading the story of Moses was the beginning of a series of exciting discoveries that would lead me to put God's promises to the test, help me to learn that God is faithful, and to see that He is ready and willing to demonstrate His relevance.

My children, Mathieu, Jenae, and Elise, were the catalyst that drove me to put God to the test. I've shunned the weekly routine of Christianity. In its place, I've desired my kids to develop their own dynamic relationship of faith, sharing, and worship. This is a journey that is far from over. Do I have the answers? Absolutely not! It's been a quest for discovery that has opened my eyes in ways that I could have never imagined. Their contribution to my life has driven me on this journey. My prayer is that each of them will take what I've learned and develop a relationship with our heavenly Father far beyond anything I will experience.

This journey would not have been possible without my wife, Linda. With each step I asked God to use her to make clear the path we should take. I praise God that she allowed the Lord to use her. She's not comfortable with risk, and stepping out in faith requires taking risks. But her willingness to be used is a testimony to God's faithfulness and goodness. More than once, when my steps faltered and I considered not moving forward, Linda reminded me of how God had worked in the past and insisted that I keep going. Often it's the small, seemingly insignificant moments that are momentous.

If it weren't for the persistence of my friends Ray and Nigel, I would never have written this book. I'm not a writer. Ray lives in Koloa, Hawaii, and Nigel lives in Abbotsford, British Columbia, Canada. The question I repeatedly asked them was, "What makes you think I have anything so special that it justifies being written?" They tackled me independently but simultaneously. Their persistence broke down my stubborn resistance.

I've enjoyed watching people discover a fresh view of our heavenly Father, which causes them to trust Him, claim His promises, and experience His faithfulness. That was why this book was written.

Writing my thoughts was the easy part; however, I needed someone who could review my work, challenge me, point out inconsistencies, and catch grammatical errors. God provided a wonderful gift through my long-time friend from high school, Della. Four times, I sent my final draft for her to read. Without being asked, she honestly edited my work and sent it back to me to review, rethink, clarify, and correct. This truly was a labor of love. I am grateful for her honesty, commitment, and encouragement.

One editor is never enough. Kris added a fresh look, reorganized my thoughts, and pushed me to add more of myself. Her goal was to ensure that each chapter was engaging and relevant for you. We spent many exhausting hours reviewing the Deuteronomy Study Guide and creating thought-provoking questions that we hope will assist you in creating a dynamic Bible study group. Lord willing, it was time well spent!

These individuals have been instruments in God's hand to shape who I am. For this, I am grateful to them and to God. He provides what we need exactly when we need it. He is faithful!

Introduction

We live in an age of dramatically increased technological advances that create opportunities for us to live longer, enjoy more free time, and increase our productivity. We thought this would enable us to enjoy more leisure time; more free time might cause us to build closer relationships. What a joke! Instead, we struggle to manage these advances. Many of us have become more isolated. Marriages struggle, people feel less connected, and children grow up feeling isolated. Technology becomes our tool to hide, to avoid being vulnerable, and to miss the joy of intimacy.

For many, we are more hurried and more stressed today than our parents or grandparents were in their day. Our career success depends on our ability to learn more, to learn it more quickly, and to embrace change at a seemingly ever-quickening pace. Our increased struggle to stay ahead has caused us to fall behind in our personal relationships and in our health. We struggle to master what used to be considered simple—the interpersonal skills needed to create, maintain, and enjoy intimacy with those closest to us. We now accept diseases of affluence as a natural part of life, even though we could avoid them altogether. Instead of life becoming simpler, it seems it has become more complex.

For those of us who believe in a loving heavenly Father, where does God fit into this picture? What's His relevance? How do our lives compare with unbelievers' lives? What tangible evidence can they *see* that our belief in God makes a significant difference in the quality of our decisions, our temperament, or our response to everyday challenges? Are we tolerant, patient, and empathetic with those around us? Are our marriages and relationships with our children happier and stronger? Regardless of our education, are we more financially secure? Are we more confident in our life journeys? What's God done in our lives this last week that excites us? What do we have to share?

In short, are we happier? Our witness is not the strength of our doctrine but the power of God exhibited in our lives. Am I saying that doctrine is not important? No. Our beliefs should make us see God more clearly and allow us to grasp God's hand and claim His power in our lives. The more we understand God, the more we'll understand what He wants to do in our lives. Our clearer picture of Him will cause us to step out in faith, claim His promises, and experience His glory. The more He works powerfully in our lives, the more we will have a testimony of relevance that people will want to hear. Let's broaden our dialogue about God and disengage from the five-hundred-year-old argument about how we make it to heaven. God wants to demonstrate His relevance by solving our problems today.

As Christians, we are to be a living testimony that, indeed, "God's promises can never fail." We are "encouraged" and "called" to *know* firsthand that, no matter the situation, our God "never sleeps and never slumbers." He's a continual partner, guiding and directing our every step. This was Moses' experience. At the end of his life, he shared with the children of Israel one of his last conversations with God. He said, "It was then I made this plea to the LORD: 'LORD God, I said, you have begun to show to your servant your great power and your strong hand: what god is there in heaven or on earth who can match your works and mighty deeds?'" (Deuteronomy 3:23, 24).

Moses was living with a daily air of expectation, awe, and thanksgiving! Despite his daunting task of guiding two million complaining, fearful, and disobedient people across the desert for forty years, he wasn't tired. He wasn't ready for retirement. Moses didn't know anything about just putting up with life. He fully embraced his task. He asked God to be his partner, and God didn't let him down. Death was the furthest thought from his mind. No matter the seemingly insurmountable difficulty, he excitedly looked forward to seeing how God would get them out of their fix. He anticipated seeing God's precious promises fulfilled. God denied Moses' expectations only once—when God wouldn't allow him to enter the Promised Land. Moses didn't know that God had something better in store for him: He was laid to rest, only to be resurrected and taken to heaven. What a punishment!

Tragically, we inadvertently miss the joy of intimacy with God. We often treat Him like He's there just to give us what we want when we want it. It's like we're spoiled children of a multibillionaire. We've missed the beauty and power of what faith can bring into our daily experience. Instead, our experience is frequently driven by a selfish focus on either going to heaven or avoiding death. We're confused. We fearfully or begrudgingly follow His counsel just so we can get a piece of our promised inheritance: heaven. Others of us think following His counsel doesn't matter. Our idea of faith and grace is that God accepts us, forgives us just as we are, and will someday change us into His image. As if there's no other option, we happily accept our limitations. We have not experienced God powerfully, answering the question: "Is there a limit to the power of the LORD? You will now see whether or not my words come true" (Numbers 11:23). Furthermore, we do not expect to see God's powerful answer. Moses always saw God's words come true; so can we. Too many of us believe that following God means sacrificing today's joy so we can go to heaven in the future. Why should an unbeliever want to join this confusion? Why should our children want to follow these footsteps?

Too often our walk with God is limited to a weekly confession of our faith. Our prayers do not reach out and claim His promises for dealing with today's challenges. We expect little, and therefore we are confirmed in our minimalist expectations. To the outside observer, such an experience holds no attraction. And why should it! There is virtually no difference in the way we live compared to those who make no apologies for wanting nothing to do with God. This should not be! Israel's complacent view of God is the experience of many of us. Zephaniah explains,

> At that time I shall search Jerusalem by lantern-light and
> punish all who are ruined by complacency like wine left
> on its lees, who say to themselves, 'The LORD will do
> nothing, neither good nor bad.' Zephaniah 1:12

We're missing out on the best part of life: getting to know Him, personally *knowing* that He loves us, seeing His promises come alive, seeing His deliverance heal us of our scars, seeing Him open and close doors, and knowing without a doubt that the path that God chooses for us *will* bring the greatest joy into our life.

When we come into God's presence, complacency is impossible. We're moved either one way or the other. It's only possible to be lukewarm if there are no encounters. Over and over again, those who witnessed Jesus performing the works of our Father were either in awe or were determined to rid themselves of Him.

Over the past ten years, God has placed me on an exciting journey of rediscovery. My rediscovery of Scripture has tested many of my cultural beliefs and opened new doors that I had overlooked or never even considered. The book of Deuteronomy transformed my view of God. It's one of the most frequently quoted books in Scripture, yet few of us have discovered its promises, its power, and its joy. Once I understood the real message of Deuteronomy, it transformed my perspective on all the other books of Scripture. I now find hidden gems everywhere. Most importantly, it's been exciting to see God transform lives through this message.

My journey has brought me to new discoveries that I had not learned from my parents or from my pastors. Each truth was found in Scripture, like jewels just waiting to be found and claimed. It has changed my life. However, I'm far from finished. It is my hope that these gems of truth will transform your life, too, bringing you a renewed sense of God's relevance, giving you a deeper love, and helping you to experience the promise of His joy—a joy that He longs to give each of us.

As you begin reading, understand that I am not trying to convince you of God's existence or the effectiveness of prayer. If you haven't already come to these conclusions, my hope is that the perspective presented will provide you with a new frame of reference. This book is simply a chronicle of my own personal discovery of overlooked, hidden gems and the impact these discoveries have had on my view of God.

In short, I've learned that it's all about trust. He asks us to take steps into the unknown to demonstrate His unfailing love and compassion.

My prayer is that you'll learn to recognize His voice and discover new dimensions of His grace. You will be thrilled as you come to *know* how much He loves you, discover how He guides you, and learn how His grace protects, elevates, heals, and enables you to reach out and touch the lives of those around you. God will be blessed as you praise the wonderful acts that He will perform in your life as you progressively learn to trust Him. May this experience be your first step in fulfillment of Isaiah 55:2: "Listen to me and you will fare well, you will enjoy the fat of the land. Come to me and listen to my words, hear me and you will have life: I shall make an everlasting covenant with you to love you faithfully as I loved David."

Chapter 1

Dreaming the Big Dream

 Hidden Gem:

"For I know the plans I have for you," says the LORD. "They are plans for good and not for disaster, to give you a future and a hope." (Jeremiah 29:11 NLT)

God gave me a dream. I let it die. That could have been the end of the story. But God didn't forget the dream He gave me. He started me on an incredible journey of faith that I am still traveling. I've been watching Him resurrect a dream that I'd long ago forgotten. Although my dream was resurrected in adversity, I've seen God repeatedly demonstrate His relevance through both the good times and the hard times of my life. He has always provided what I and my family needed when we needed it. Yet I'm currently unemployed, and my heart struggles with bouts of anxiety, wondering how He's going to provide for us this time. But through these hard times, God is slowly fulfilling the dream, and it is even bigger and more amazing than I imagined. It is a dream that totally brings glory to God.

When I decided to pursue my Masters in Business Administration (MBA), I wanted to do something to positively impact people's lives, to use my talent in financial things to help people who might not be as knowledgeable about managing their finances. I didn't know

1

exactly how I would be able to do this, but that was the essence of the dream. When I graduated with my MBA, I chose to work in healthcare administration, but I soon learned it provided little room to make a positive difference. The business world is all about the bottom line.

When I married Linda and our three children entered our lives, my focus was to provide for my family. The responsibilities of earning a living and caring for a family left no room for abstract ideas. I had no time to pursue unfulfilled dreams. Consequently, my dream died and was soon forgotten. What's exciting is that the Lord remembered it. Unbeknownst to me, he was orchestrating events in my life to resurrect it. As my journey progressed, He has given me new gifts. Each gift has required that I step out in faith. It's never been easy and, ironically, it has not gotten any easier with time. God keeps raising the bar! However, as I've continued on this journey, I've experienced increasing feelings of anticipation and gratefulness.

There have been many instances of faith-building events in my life, some of which I will share with you later. But I will start with the events that led directly to the rebirth of my dream. My family and I moved to Washington State from Hawaii. Almost a year and a half after moving to Bellingham, Washington, I was hired by the owner of a company whose primary business was operating long-term care facilities. As a short-term commitment, I assumed management of his mortgage company just as the sub-prime mortgage meltdown began. What great timing! The company had never made a penny of profit. We both knew that it would be a real challenge to make it profitable now; however, before closing the company we wanted to give it one last chance. If things didn't work out with the mortgage company, I was told there would be other opportunities available within the company for me.

After three years of twelve- to fourteen-hour work days, plus a minimum three-hour daily commute, it was clear that we'd done everything possible and it was time to close the business. However, after the devastating impact of the mortgage mess, the other opportunities available to me in the company had all dried up. Consequently, I recommended to my boss that I be laid off effective June 1, 2009. I had no job leads and had yet to develop much of a business network. It appeared that the move to Washington with my family had killed my career.

Little did I realize that many of the disasters I experienced would actually resurrect my dream.

I had never worked so hard at a job. But now I had absolutely nothing to show for my efforts. To say the least, I was very discouraged! I'd never worked in an industry that didn't understand the basic concepts of customer service, excellence, honesty, and teamwork.

Nevertheless, from this experience, God orchestrated events to give me insight into a little noticed financial tool that can save people thousands of dollars. How did I know the insight was a gift from God? At first, I didn't recognize it; however, as I showed the concept to very smart, reputable finance professionals, I repeatedly saw that they had overlooked it, too. The one person who understood it and applied it couldn't see how to use it to make any money. If these seasoned professionals didn't understand it, why would I—an individual new to the field—pick it up in just six months? That's why I consider it a gift from God.

The overlooked tool is the average daily balance. I learned about this remarkable financial tool inadvertently. This came about when circumstances led to my physical absence from one office for three months. During this time, Macquarie Bank (from Australia) included our mortgage company in one of their exclusive contracts. Mind you, if I had been present at the office, the discussions would have included more conservative estimates of the company's projected growth so that, in all probability, the bank would not have contracted with the mortgage company at all. Nevertheless, as a result of this contract, I learned how managing your average daily balance can save thousands of dollars. Understanding this enabled me to develop my financial model.

When the Macquarie bank representative visited the mortgage company to train the loan officers. His opening comments were, "How would you like to show your clients how to pay off their mortgage in half the time without changing their spending? Using this product, the interest rate doesn't matter."

This sounded like a scam! As I listened to him and began testing a couple of scenarios, I confirmed that he was telling the truth. I was amazed.

Using Microsoft Excel software, I developed a training module for loan officers and clients so they could understand the concept.

Unfortunately, during this time, Macquarie Bank closed their operations in the United States because of the deepening mortgage crisis. It appeared that my work had been a waste of time. But a couple of months later, a friend called me repeatedly, urging me to develop it into an online teaching tool. He persistently called me every couple of weeks for three months before I relented. I began developing the teaching tool while still working for the company.

When the economy finally crippled the company to the point where I resigned, I decided to take the tool God had helped me discover and develop it into a product that could be of benefit to others. This product would be available on the iPad and have two applications: a free "app" that anyone could access and a more detailed product that could be purchased. Although I had little capital, God brought the right people to my help at just the right time. For example, a gifted engineer/programmer provided tremendous counsel in developing an educational video; the owner of another software company showed up at just the right time to provide the guidance necessary to develop an iPad application; and a local bank executive promoted the product among his clients.

At each step of the way, I saw God's gifts to me. For example, as I began building the spreadsheet prototype, I needed certain solutions, but didn't know the appropriate Excel command. So, I called the Microsoft Excel help line. I was told that because this was a business application, I needed to call another department. I was warned that they would probably charge me $500. When I called, I was told that since I'd just purchased Excel for Mac, they would assist me at no cost. Ten hours later, I had my solution free of charge. What a blessing!

Another time, a church friend introduced me to his next-door neighbor, an executive of Apple. The executive reviewed my Excel worksheet and encouraged me to create an iPhone application. He referred me to an independent software engineer in Ottawa, Ontario. He's a very gifted man who has done great work for some very large corporations and specializes in developing Apple iPhone applications. He didn't need my business; however, he understood the concept and was excited about helping people achieve their financial goals. He provided hours of invaluable assistance that significantly reduced my development costs.

Another interesting outcome came from a client case that I had assumed from a negligent loan officer while I was still working for the mortgage company. This situation required that I pick up the pieces. I proposed a solution that could save the customer over $400,000 in interest payments; however, he needed a line of credit. After failing to get approval from two different banks, I introduced myself to the branch manager of another large regional bank. I explained how I was trying to assist the customer using this unique solution.

The branch manager was all too glad to help. She submitted my proposed solution with the client's application and the bank's underwriting department approved the line of credit. The branch manager was impressed with the borrower's excitement over the innovative solution I'd provided, his willingness to participate in several other bank products, and the strong personal commitment that he showed towards the bank. In the branch manager's 30 years, she had never witnessed such enthusiasm. The customer was so satisfied with the service provided by the bank and with my solution, he's repeatedly volunteered to provide testimonials.

The bank asked me to conduct seminars at their Bellingham branch to see if this experience could easily be replicated. Each of the attendees at the first session was excited about the concepts and would have bought the application if it had been ready. Then a CPA who attended the seminar asked me to share the information with his high net-worth clients. No hard selling was necessary.

These outcomes have just fallen into my lap like ripe fruit falling from a tree. It's been amazing how God has worked.

After I became unemployed I was able to develop educational videos, marketing, and employee training materials for this product. If I'd still been working full time, I would not have been able to develop the materials needed to create a credible business plan and presentation for the bank. My heart is filled with such gratitude and praise for God's goodness.

My dream has the real possibility of being bigger than I'd ever thought possible. My product, CashMap, an educational, interactive finance iPad application, is now available to help people save thousands of dollars in interest, pay off their loans faster, and boost their savings. In addition, God has cared financially for my own family, grown my faith, and, through my circumstances, revealed Himself to those who assisted me along the way. I can take no credit for what's happened. The events leading me to this point all seemed to spring from disappointing circumstances. But God took those disappointments and turned them into something that would reveal His power and glory.

While studying for my MBA twenty-eight years ago, I had a dream of using my talents to help people with their finances. It was a pleasant shock when I realized that God had not forgotten my dream. All of my experiences over the past many years have contributed to growing the skills I needed to successfully accomplish my dream. God knew what He was doing even though I didn't have a clue.

We have all probably asked this question at some time in our lives: "What exactly is God's vision for my life?" God desires to take us from wherever we are and restore us to His image. This means there is no such thing as "can't"! *Joyful obedience to God's counsel unleashes God's wonderful grace, which transforms us and starts us on a lifetime journey of achievement.*

God wants us to dream. He both respects and inspires our dreams. I don't yet understand how this dynamic works. Scripture reflects examples of both. I do know that, in either case, the individual embarks on a wonderful life journey that enriches both his life and the lives of those around him. He lives a life full of purpose. There is an excitement and an anticipation about seeing what God will do next. This was Moses' experience and why He pled with God to allow him to see the Promised Land. In Deuteronomy 3:24, he says, "O Sovereign LORD, you have only begun to show me your greatness and power. Is there any god in heaven or on earth who can perform such great deeds as yours?" (NLT).

This is the experience that God invites us all to know: to dream, to commit, and then to step out in faith. Imagine what would have happened if Abraham hadn't left his home, if Nehemiah had waited for someone else to rebuild Jerusalem's wall, if David hadn't volunteered to kill Goliath, if Elijah hadn't demanded that God heal the widow's son, if Hezekiah hadn't asked God to heal the people, or if Paul and Silas hadn't sung songs of praise while in prison. Each one had a dream that became a passion. This, too, is our calling.

God took Abram outside and said, "'Look up at the sky and count the stars, if you can. So many will your descendants be.' Abram put his faith in the LORD, who reckoned it to him as righteousness" (Genesis 15:5–6).

Frequently, our dreams are God's still, small voice speaking to us. God has no interest in us going through life with a melancholy spirit. He wants us to dream big! Besides Abram, think about Jabez who specifically asked that God grant him wide territories. Moses, remembering the promise given to Abraham, dreamed of the day Israel would be liberated from slavery. Each one had a passion that they committed to the Lord.

Rediscovering our passion, learning to dream, and committing our plans to the Lord allows His grace to open our eyes so we can see the next steps we need to take and the personal victories we must achieve. With each step, we feel a greater need for God to work in our lives.

Unfortunately, I've not seen many people take these steps. Instead, I've heard countless people say, "I want to serve God, but God hasn't shown me what I should do," or, "I don't have any talents." David writes in Psalm 139:13–15:

> You it was who fashioned my inward parts; you knitted me together in my mother's womb. I praise you, for you fill me with awe; wonderful you are, and wonderful your works. You know me through and through: my body was no mystery to you, when I was formed in secret, woven in the depths of the earth.

Each of us has a unique combination of talents. Our first challenge is to learn to trust God, believing He has something special planned that will excite us. He is actively guiding each chapter of our lives, no matter how unpleasant the current chapter may be. We need to remember the promise given in Jeremiah 29:11: "I alone know my purpose for you, says the LORD: wellbeing and not misfortune, and a long line of descendants after you." We can then dream and share with God what excites us.

Trust, plan, commit, trust, and then act. This cycle is to be continually repeated. Serving God is not limited to being a pastor, missionary, or medical professional. There are so many ways to enrich the lives of the people with whom you come in contact. Start dreaming;

don't create limits. When we place limits on ourselves, we place limits on God's ability to act, which is directly tied to our faith.

Let's review some of the key elements of this process.

1. **The Plan:** Our passion, coupled with faith in God's promises, grants us the courage to pursue and achieve our uniquely personal dreams. Personal growth, united with experiencing God's care, ignites a spirit of joy and gratitude.

   > The LORD, your Redeemer, the Holy One of Israel, says: "I am the Lord your God, who teaches you what is good and leads you along the paths you should follow." (Isaiah 48:17 NLT)

   > Commit to the LORD all that you do, and your plans will be successful. (Proverbs 16:3)

2. **The Next Step:** He helps us make wise decisions and to grow. He provides our needs at just the right time. This brings personal growth, which encourages a spirit of discovery. Bad habits, self-defeating thoughts, and fears are our biggest challenges to achieving our dreams. We move forward in a series of small steps. We rejoice over the doors God opens and the healthy habits we develop; these enable us to continue moving forward. We experience His deliverance and healing from poor choices, emotional scars, and bad habits, and this helps us love others in a spirit of empathy and patience. This is God's grace in action.

   > It is **the LORD who bestows wisdom and teaches knowledge and understanding. Out of his store he endows the upright with ability.** For those whose conduct is blameless he is shield, guarding the course of justice and keeping watch over the way of his loyal servants. (Proverbs 2:6–8, emphasis supplied)

   > Even before they call to me, I shall answer, and while they are still speaking I shall respond. (Isaiah 65:24)

   > If you call to me I shall answer, and tell you great and mysterious things of which you are still unaware. (Jeremiah 33:3)

3. **The Victory:** God provides answers to the hurdles we face and brings us to places we never anticipated. This journey brings us joy and displaces fear. We plan and move forward, no longer allowing fear to paralyze us. Just as God spoke to Moses and Jeremiah, we too will hear His voice with each new mountain: "I am the LORD, the God of all mankind; is anything impossible for me?" (Jeremiah 32:27). We learn to patiently wait for God to open the next door. We learn that He's never too slow; He provides what's needed at just the right time. The lesson taught in Isaiah 30:15—"In calm detachment lies your safety, your strength in quiet trust"—becomes a reality. "Yet the LORD is waiting to show you his favour, and he yearns to have pity on you; for the LORD is a God of justice. Happy are all who wait for him!" (verse 18). Once we learn this lesson, our confidence in God grows and we can trust Him further. This also strengthens our bonds of intimacy with our heavenly Father, our spouse, and with those on a similar walk. Our spirit of gratitude ignites a spirit of generosity.

> I have come that they may have life, and may have it in all its fullness...I am the good shepherd; I know my own and my own know me, as the Father knows me and I know the Father. (John 10:10,14)

> In a word, as God's dear children, you must be like him. Live in love as Christ loved you and gave himself up on your behalf. (Ephesians 5:1–2)

Each of these steps contributes to both achieving our dream and living the abundant life that God has promised. Let's look at the lives of a couple of individuals who realized their dream. The outcome exceeded their wildest imagination. Let's start with David.

As a boy, David learned to trust God with the simplest things of life. Most of us go through life never learning to develop such a simple trust. Unfortunately, Scripture doesn't give us any insight as to how he learned to do this. It's also clear that none of his brothers learned to trust God like their youngest brother. When Israel was in their face-off against Goliath and the Philistines, look at David's confidence of victory when he speaks to King Saul:

David said to Saul, 'Sir, I am my father's shepherd; whenever a lion or bear comes and carries off a sheep from the flock, I go out after it and attack it and rescue the victim from its jaws. Then if it turns on me, I seize it by the beard and batter it to death. I have killed lions and bears, and this uncircumcised Philistine will fare no better than they; he has defied the ranks of the living God. The Lord who saved me from the lion and the bear will save me from this Philistine.'"(1 Samuel 17:34–36)

I don't think it is commonplace for shepherds to wrestle sheep from the jaws of a lion or a bear and then seize it by the head and batter it to death. David's response was immediate and spontaneous! He didn't ask for a season of prayer. By experience, he had learned God's protection. Such a reaction does not come from head knowledge. It comes only from experiences that are validated over and over again. Not many people have learned to trust God and experience His power. A trusting relationship is precious in God's eyes. So precious, in fact, that He chose David to rule Israel.

Although anointed to be King of Israel as a teenager (this was God's dream for him), David ran from King Saul for years before this dream *finally* became a reality. Despite having multiple opportunities to kill King Saul, David maintained his trust in God. He allowed God to work things out in His way and at His time.

When he finally became king of Israel, his heart was full of gratitude for what God had done. He looked at his palace and told Nathan the prophet; "'Here I am living in a house of cedar, while the Ark of the Covenant of the LORD is housed in a tent'" (1 Chronicles 17:1). David realized that God deserved to be in a place befitting a God that had so wonderfully delivered, guided, and established him as King over Israel. I found God's response to Nathan a bit surprising:

'Go and say to David my servant, This is the word of the LORD: It is not you who are to build me a house to dwell in. Down to this day I have never dwelt in a house since I brought Israel up from Egypt; I lived in a tent and a tabernacle. Wherever I journeyed with Israel, did I ever ask any of the judges whom I appointed shepherds

of my people why they had not built me a cedar house?'
(1 Chronicles 17:4)

Dwelling in a temple was not God's dream; it was David's. However, because David's request was a response to God's goodness, his request was accepted with one condition: David's son would build the temple. Even better, God gave David another promise in 1 Chronicles 17:13: "'I shall be a father to him, and he will be my son. I shall never withdraw my love from him as I withdrew it from your predecessor. But I shall give him a sure place in my house and kingdom for all time, and his throne will endure forever.'"

David was awed and humbled by God's overwhelming generosity in answering a request that wasn't even His dream. David responds in verses 16–19:

> 'Who am I, LORD God, and what is my family, that you have brought me thus far? It was a small thing in your sight, God, to have planned for your servant's house in days long past, and now you look on me as a man already embarked on a high career, LORD God. What more can David say to you of the honour you have done your servant? You yourself know your servant. For the sake of your servant, LORD, in accordance with your purpose, you have done this great thing and revealed all the great things to come.'

All this came from a dream that was born out of gratitude and awe for the things that God had done in David's life! And how did it all begin? David made the choice to trust in God during the simple, and probably boring, task of faithfully tending to his father's sheep! He could have let a lion or bear have the sheep, but David asked for God's help. David wanted to do his best.

We know God accepted David's vision as His own. In David's final counsel to Solomon he said, "'All this was **drafted by the LORD's own hand**,' said David; 'my part was to consider the detailed working out of the plan'" (1 Chronicles 28:19, emphasis supplied).

God gives to Isaiah the same promise that He repeatedly gave to Moses:

Come for water, all who are thirsty; though you have no money, come, buy grain and eat; come, buy wine and milk, not for money, not for a price. Why spend your money for what is not food, your earnings on what fails to satisfy? **Listen to me and you will fare well, you will enjoy the fat of the land.** Come to me and **listen to my words, hear me and you will have life: I shall make an everlasting covenant with you to love you faithfully as I loved David**. I appointed him a witness to peoples, a prince ruling over them; and **you in turn will summon nations you do not know, and nations that do not know you will hasten to you, because the LORD your God, Israel's Holy One, has made you glorious.** (Isaiah 55:1–5, emphasis supplied)

God tried to help Israel understand that He is not bound by limitations:

For my thoughts are not your thoughts, nor are your ways my ways. This is the word of the LORD. But as the heavens are high above the earth, so are my ways high above your ways and my thoughts above your thoughts. As the rain and snow come down from the heavens and do not return there without watering the earth, making it produce grain to give seed for sowing and bread to eat, so is it with my word issuing from my mouth; it will not return to me empty without accomplishing my purpose and succeeding in the task for which I sent it. (Isaiah 55:8–11)

Years later, Paul repeats the same promise:

I speak God's hidden wisdom, his secret purpose framed from the very beginning to bring us to our destined glory....Scripture speaks of '**things beyond our seeing, things beyond our hearing, things beyond our imagining,** all prepared by God for those who love him.' (1 Corinthians 2:7, 9, emphasis supplied)

These promises are ours too! God uses David as an example of the kind of relationship He'd like to enjoy with us. Begin dreaming and present it to the Lord. He has something exciting in mind!

David's story continues with his son, Solomon. We know nothing about how prepared he was to rule the nation or what his natural talents were before he became king. We do know that he felt totally overwhelmed by the challenges that lay ahead of him. He doubted His ability to fill his father's shoes. Listen to Solomon's humble prayer:

> Now, LORD my God, you have made your servant king in place of my father David, though I am a mere child, unskilled in leadership. Here I am in the midst of your people, the people of your choice, too many to be numbered or counted. Grant your servant, therefore, a heart with skill to listen, so that he may govern your people justly and distinguish good from evil. Otherwise who is equal to the task of governing this great people of yours? (1 Kings 3:7–9)

Note God's generous response to Solomon's request:

> And God said, 'Because you have asked for this, and not for long life, or for wealth, or for the lives of your enemies, but have asked for discernment in administering justice, I grant your request; I give you a heart so wise and so understanding that there has been none like you before your time, nor will there be after you. What is more, I give you those things for which you did not ask, such wealth and glory as no king of your time can match. If you conform to my ways and observe my ordinances and commandments, as your father David did, I will also give you long life.' (1 Kings 3:11–14)

God is reassuring Solomon and adding a few new elements. Besides promising unprecedented wealth, God repeats the promise given to Moses that following God's ordinances and commandments would bring the blessing of a long life. In Solomon's early years, he faithfully trusted the Lord. During those years, Solomon enjoyed unparalleled wealth and emotionally fulfilling relationships both at home and with those who worked for him.

Upon hearing wonderful reports about Solomon, the Queen of Sheba felt compelled to come and see it for herself. Chapter 9 of 2 Chronicles tells of her visit. "The Queen of Sheba heard of Solomon's fame and came to test him with enigmatic questions" (verse 1). Her response says much about what God wants to do in our lives and the impact we will have on those with whom we come in contact. She certainly found him to be smart enough, for "Solomon answered all her questions; not one of them was too hard for him to answer" (2 Chronicles 9:2). But this wasn't what impressed her the most.

> She was overcome with amazement. She said to the king, 'The account which I heard in my own country about your achievements and your wisdom was true, but I did not believe what they told me until I came and saw for myself. Indeed, I was not told half of the greatness of your wisdom; you surpass all I had heard of you. **Happy are your wives, happy these courtiers of yours who are in attendance on you every day** and hear your wisdom! Blessed be the LORD your God who has delighted in you and has set you on his throne as his king; because in his love your God has elected Israel to make it endure forever, he has made you king over it to maintain law and justice." (2 Chronicles 9:4–6)

It was the quality of Solomon's relationships that impressed her the most. She was also impressed with God working through Solomon to maintain law and justice. When the temple was completed, Solomon rejoiced over God's goodness and requested His continued grace. He prayed,

> Blessed be the LORD who has given his people Israel rest, as he promised: not one of the promises he made through his servant Moses has failed. May the LORD our God be with us as he was with our forefathers; may he never leave us or forsake us. May he turn our hearts towards him, so that we may conform to all his ways, observing his commandments, statutes, and judgments, as he commanded our forefathers....So all the peoples of the

earth will know that the LORD is God, he and no other.
(1 Kings 8:56–58, 60)

God fulfills His promises and our dreams so that those around us will know God is actively at work. This is His way of demonstrating His relevance. He doesn't act arbitrarily. He even works upon the hearts of others to help. When Solomon asked for help from King Hiram of Tyre, Hiram responded,

> 'It is because of the love which the Lord has for his people that he has made you king over them.' The letter continued, 'Blessed be the LORD the God of Israel, maker of heaven and earth, who has given to King David a wise son, endowed with insight and understanding, to build a house for the LORD and a royal palace for himself.' (2 Chronicles 2:11–12)

God opened the door and made sure that David's dream came true.

Let's look at another example: Jesus' disciples. First, let's consider how Jesus recruited Peter by acting powerfully and fulfilling a dream beyond his wildest imaginings. We'll then look at the impact Jesus had on him.

Jesus recruited Peter by bringing phenomenal results to the rather routine day of a fisherman. In Luke 5, we read about a miracle so overwhelming that Peter was moved to take action. He had been out fishing all night and had caught nothing. Jesus found him in a group of fishermen cleaning their nets. He approached and asked him to go back out and cast his net in deeper waters. Peter could have said, "Forget it! I'm tired, and I've had enough. I'm not going back out there on your wishful thinking!" Instead, in an act of faith, Peter went back out and started fishing. He caught so many fish that it split his nets, and he yelled for James and John to help him. Soon both boats were filled with fish—to the point that they were on the verge of sinking!

Jesus made an immediate, dramatic impact. Peter experienced a big fish story that exceeded his wildest dreams. Only after Jesus demonstrated God's relevance did He talk to Peter about the future. But Peter's dream of catching fish no longer captured his imagination. Peter was ready to move on to a bigger dream.

Knowing that God was present, Peter felt unworthy. He turned to Jesus, fell on his knees, and said, "'Go, Lord, leave me, sinner that I am!'" (Luke 5:8). There was no doubt in Peter's mind that Jesus had a vision for his life. "As soon as they had brought the boats to land, they left everything and followed him" (verse 11). God desires to work in our lives in dramatic ways that leave no doubt about His dreams for us.

After Jesus ascended to heaven, we see the transforming effect Jesus had on Peter and John. Acts 4:13 shows how the high priests reacted to the transformation of Peter and John: "Observing that Peter and John were uneducated laymen, they were astonished at their boldness and took note that they had been companions of Jesus." Peter and John replied to the Jewish rulers, elders, and scribes, "'Is it right in the eyes of God for us to obey you rather than him? Judge for yourselves. We cannot possibly give up speaking about what we have seen and heard'" (Acts 4:19–20).

It's the same story today. When God is permitted to act, He acts dramatically. God transforms both the individual acting in faith and the people who witness His power. We see the results of joyfully embracing God's counsel and being in His presence. Dreams are fulfilled and new dreams are created. This is the consistent message of both the Old and New Testaments.

Our lives are all about dealing with day-to-day challenges. God's focus has always been to walk with us, to provide the help we need, and to fill our hearts with praise. Just before the Lord's Prayer, it says, "In your prayers do not go babbling on like the heathen, who imagine that the more they say the more likely they are to be heard. Do not imitate them, for your Father knows what your needs are before you ask him" (Matthew 6:7). Spend a few moments thinking about that verse—this also means that He knows what we need *before* we know we need it!

God's message is consistent. He wants to transform us. He wants to partner with us in creating dreams and honoring our dreams. For those who learn to trust Him, obstacles are turned into dramatic examples of God's faithfulness and love for us. Abraham saw the first glimpse of the promise God gave him, Joseph became the second most powerful individual in Egypt, Moses realized his dream of liberating Israel from slavery, and David saw the detailed vision of the temple that would be built following his death. Each of these dreams took years to achieve.

Each person's willingness to partner with God to achieve the seemingly impossible was counted by God as righteousness. Their willingness to partner with God in the present ensured their eternal walk with their Creator. This, too, is our calling.

Jesus makes it clear that God wants to experience the same intimate relationship with us as Jesus shares with Him. Jesus is our example. As God directed Jesus' journey, He desires to direct ours. "'He who sent me is present with me, and has not left me on my own; for I always do what is pleasing to him'" (John 8:29). Note the similarity to our calling. "Jesus replied, 'Anyone who loves me will heed what I say; then my Father will love him, and we will come to him and make our dwelling with him'" (John 14:23).

Let's look at another example. Jesus said of himself, "'I do not speak on my own authority, but the Father who sent me has himself commanded me what to say and how to speak. I know that his commands are eternal life. What the Father has said to me, therefore—that is what I speak" (John 12:49–50). Once again, note the similarity when Jesus says of our calling, "As you sent me into the world, I have sent them into the world, and for their sake I consecrate myself, that they too may be consecrated by the truth" (John 17:18–19).

Here's a third example: Jesus said, "Do you not believe that I am in the Father, and the Father in me? I am not myself the source of the words I speak to you: it is the Father who dwells in me doing his own work" (John 14:10–11). He then makes this striking prophecy: "In very truth I tell you, whoever has faith in me will do what I am doing; indeed he will do greater things still because I am going to the Father. Anything you ask in my name I will do, so that the Father may be glorified in the Son. If you ask anything in my name I will do it" (John 14:12–14).

Christ was a willing partner in showing us what it means to glorify God. Each day our heavenly Father directed Jesus' life. In John 12:44–46, "Jesus proclaimed: 'To believe in me, is not to believe in me but in him who sent me; to see me, is to see him who sent me. I have come into the world as light so that no one who has faith in me should remain in darkness.'" Jesus wanted us to understand that everything that God did in Jesus' life, He will do in ours. "'You are light for all the world. A town that stands on a hill cannot be hidden.…Like the lamp, you must shed light among your fellows, so that, when they see the good you do, they may give praise to your Father in heaven" (Matthew 5:14, 16).

God has a unique journey for each of us. The longer we wait to begin the journey, the more time we will have wasted. We're missing out on a journey of a lifetime. He's planted a dream in your heart, and He is waiting for you to step out in faith to fulfill that dream. Will you trust Him and begin a life of discovery?

Action Steps

1. What brings you the greatest satisfaction in life? Does it bring God glory? Are you actively engaged in this pursuit now? What more could you do to make it even more satisfying?

2. If you're unsure what's brings you satisfaction, begin your investigation by identifying your strengths. Ask a friend to help.

3. Write down the steps needed to achieve your dream. Break down the process into small, doable steps.

4. What are your obstacles? List possible solutions.

5. Are you willing to take the time to learn? What changes will be needed in your life?

6. When you visualize achieving your goal, how do you feel?

Scripture for Additional Study

Isaiah 30:15, 18–21
Psalm 25
Joshua 1:8–9
Psalm 27:14; 31:14–16; 32:6–8,11
Proverbs 10:24; 11:14; 12:1,14; 13:10–15, 18, 22; and 16:3, 9, 20

Chapter 2

Trusting God

Hidden
Gem:

But I am like an olive tree, thriving in the house of God. I trust in God's unfailing love forever and ever. (Psalm 52:8 NLT)

In order to reach the vision that God has for us, we have to trust that God will do what He says. In the beginning, I really didn't understand what it meant to trust God. I was ignorant; however, I didn't know I was ignorant. I'd gone to church every week; yet I still didn't understand. I didn't realize that believing in God and trusting in God are two entirely different things. I did not understand that trusting God means *knowing* in my heart that His ways are loving and sure. How do I gain such confidence? It comes from acting on my belief, and then experiencing God fulfilling His promises to me.

When I was living in Hawaii, I applied for a job that I thought I was perfectly suited for, although it required relocating from Kauai to Oahu. Just days before the interview, it appeared that all the doors were open. I'd been told the job was mine for the taking. However, the evening before the interview, my wife suddenly changed her mind and said she was not going to move.I had learned that the Lord can work through our spouses in giving direction, and I had seen God repeatedly work through my wife.

What was I to do? I proposed a simple solution: I would fly between the islands for the first six months and, if that didn't work out, we would then move. She agreed to my compromise.

The next day, the interview seemed to be going along nicely when I was asked if I'd be willing to relocate. I said that I would commute for the first six months, and the executive seemed fine with my response. When I left, I thought I had the job in the bag. Needless to say, I was shocked when I learned that I hadn't gotten it. I couldn't understand why God had, at the last minute, failed to answer my prayer.

A couple of days later, I spoke with another executive who expressed surprise that I didn't get the job. However, he told me that, according to the interviewer, I said I *wasn't* willing to move. I was absolutely shocked! The interviewer heard the exact opposite of what I said. You might say it was as though he had interviewed an entirely different person.

When I heard this, I knew God had intervened. Although I felt bad about not getting the job I wanted, I felt even worse for thinking that God had left me out on a limb. As time passed, I was increasingly grateful for the outcome. It seemed that the job would have brought me no personal satisfaction while causing me considerable stress. A few months later I was promoted to fill another position in my company. Ironically, in my new position, I was allowed to commute between Kauai and Oahu, which I did for the next four years. In this position, I would uncover a talent I didn't know I had—one that was a critical component of the dream God would begin fulfilling in my life years later.

Another example of my learning to trust God happened a few years after this experience. God richly rewarded my family when we left that secure and stable job on Kauai and moved to Bellingham, Washington. When we moved, I didn't have a job and I had no solid leads. Why did I do this? My wife and I wanted our children, Mathieu, Jenae, and Elise, to continue growing up surrounded by people who accepted them for who they were, and to be active participants in a healthy church and academic environment.

Many years later, my heart is filled with gratitude at seeing my children develop into happy, mature adults. They love the Lord and have begun their own journey of service. God did not provide all the answers before we took the first step. We had to take one step at a time. This is what makes faith so difficult. He opens one door at a time. He doesn't give us the entire picture.

The verses I've clung to are found in Matthew 6:31–34.

> Do not ask anxiously, "What are we to eat? What are
> we to drink? What shall we wear?" These are the things
> that occupy the minds of the heathen, but your heavenly
> Father knows that you need them all. Set your mind on
> God's kingdom and his justice before everything else, and
> all the rest will come to you as well. So do not be anxious
> about tomorrow; tomorrow will look after itself. Each day
> has troubles enough of its own.

After being in Bellingham for a year, I finally got a job. But this position had its difficulties as well, and, a few years later, I found myself unemployed again. This time I began to work on the dream that God had put in my heart. While I don't know anyone that looks forward to being unemployed, I've received tremendous blessings that developed my faith in God's ability to provide for my family and me. For example, in a wonderful answer to prayer, monies owed us were repaid—money I had come to believe I would never see again. To add to the blessing, the additional funds necessary to meet our daily needs and keep our daughter in college also materialized. The additional dollars came in the form of an unexpected surge in the value of my retirement fund.

After almost three years of long hours away from home, this time of unemployment has been a wonderful time to recharge my battery and strengthen my relationships with my wife and daughter. While looking for work is stressful, the benefits of being with the family have been wonderful.

We are told that we should love God because He first loved us—that He sent His Son to the world to die for our sins so that we might be saved and have eternal life. For me, this explanation was incomplete. It just wasn't enough. It never created the emotional connection for me that it has for others. I needed my own personal story. I wasn't entirely sure what was missing, so I didn't know how to fill in the gaps.

Eternal life is great, but I spent most of my time dealing with the relentless day-to-day challenges! Recognizing that we live in a terrible world marked by man's inhumanity to his fellow man, I'd come to accept these challenges as something I simply had to put up with while trying not to be a part of the problem. Of course that's easier said than done. However, I couldn't help but ask, Where does God fit into meeting my everyday challenges? Simply "putting up" with challenges did nothing toward giving me a reason to trust God.

As a father, I tried to actively help each of my children. What did my heavenly Father want to do in my life? What were His intentions? What was I missing?

The question of trust *is* the key issue for both us and God. There's really nothing else. When Satan first spoke with Eve, he questioned whether God could be trusted. He continues to create reasons for us to doubt God. Once the issue of trust is addressed, everything else will fall into place, just like pieces to a puzzle.

Let's start with ourselves. We accept someone's advice because we believe we'll be better off. We have to know that they have our best interests at heart. If we know them, we can look at past experience to determine if we can trust them. We'll look to see if they walk the walk. We can quickly determine whether they deserve our time! If we don't know the person, we look to others whom we trust to validate that this is someone whose counsel we should follow.

Once we've made the decision to trust someone, a confidence follows that enables us to feel comfortable with their advice. Trust brings confidence. When we truly trust someone, we believe they understand us, will keep our secrets, accept us as we are, and give us sound counsel.

Of course, we've all gone through the experience of having trust broken in a relationship. Sometimes that means we become more cautious about trusting the next time—we develop a hesitancy to be vulnerable. Trust is the key component that allows us to enjoy intimacy. Developing and maintaining intimate relationships is becoming increasingly difficult. Many people come from dysfunctional parental relationships and also find themselves too busy to invest time in relationships.

Christianity's focus on heaven bypasses the joy of an intimate relationship with our God now. It also creates a challenge: none of us knows anyone who is currently experiencing eternal life. To state the obvious, eternal life is something we hope to experience someday in the future. We have no personal acquaintance with it now. We have nothing to verify it, so many people are not comfortable claiming the promise of eternal life as their own. This is why trusting God must combine our present experience with our hope for the future. Learning to trust Him with our daily challenges brings confidence that our hope of eternal life will be a reality. Without firsthand understanding that God's promises do come true, we doubt His promises for eternal life; we see it as a hollow promise. Personal experience brings us confidence about expecting eternal life.

Too often, the question of one's faith is limited to the doctrine we embrace. Our doctrine alone is not enough to strengthen our faith. Doctrine should give us a clearer view of our heavenly Father, which bolsters our confidence to claim God's promises. But it is God's personal response that really strengthens our connection with Him and demonstrates His faithfulness to us. Deepening trust in God builds our personal relationship with Him. We are all called to "taste and see that the Lord is good" (Psalm 34:8).This only comes by personal knowledge that is daily strengthened by new experiences. This makes trust dynamic and ever changing. It never stands still.

Getting to know God is like building a new friendship. God's message in both the Old Testament and the New Testament is the same. His message can be simply summarized in the following: "You *can* trust me. I want to guide you safely through this treacherous environment. All the counsel I provide is for *your* benefit. I desire an intimate relationship that will enable you to grow and experience mind-boggling things. I'm consistent, I'm patient, I'm merciful, I'm all powerful, and the very nature of my character is love. Learn to trust me by joyfully obeying my counsel and claiming my promises. This will bring you eternal life." As God told Moses, "I am that I am" (Exodus 3:14). He wants us to get started *now!*

Too often we take a limited and legalistic view of sin: it's "the transgression of the law" (I John 3:4 KJV). This is certainly accurate; however, how does the law fit in with a trusting relationship? Psalm 119:111–112 says, "Your instruction is my everlasting heritage; it is the joy of my heart. I am resolved to fulfill your statutes; they are a reward that never fails." When we understand that all God's counsel is given to bless us, it gives sin a whole new relevance in our lives. Sin is anything that gets in the way of our receiving the blessings that God has in store for us.

Stop and consider this. Sin is no longer just about what you do or say. Rather, it is also about not trusting God. It blocks you from stepping out in faith so that you can grow outside of your comfort zone. This broader view of sin forces you to toss out that checklist of static do's and don'ts! You're forced to engage with your Creator one-on-one and discover the path that He's set out for you.

Does this mean that we'll never suffer? Absolutely not, but trusting God enables Him to work in ways inconceivable to us. He promises to take the pain and turn it into something that will demonstrate His love, power, compassion, faithfulness, and mercy. When we let fear get the best of us, we're depriving ourselves of the blessing of experiencing His power, love, and faithfulness. When we don't experience His power, we're left struggling with doubt.

Satan wants to place doubts in our minds. He tells us we're all alone, that we know what's best for our own lives, that we're not good enough, that God is arbitrary and severe, that His promises don't apply to us, that He's not interested in our happiness, that we need to be practical… The list goes on and on. He'll do anything he can to create doubt.

A couple of Bible stories really drive home the point of just how difficult it has always been for us to get our head around this simple message. Even some of God's best friends struggled with this concept.

In Genesis 12, God directed Abram to leave his home and promised to make him into a great nation. He even promised that he'd be so greatly blessed that his name would be used in blessings. Abram should have been confident that God was with him, protecting him and his family. He left his home with his wife, Sarai, when he was seventy-five years old and Sarai was sixty-seven. They left and didn't know where they were going! Nevertheless, Abram feared for his life because of Sarai's beauty. He even told his wife to say that he was her brother. Sure enough, Pharaoh noticed her beauty and took her home to be his wife. God appeared to Pharaoh in a dream and told him not to touch Sarai because she was Abram's wife. How's that for God acting as a shield for both Abram and Pharaoh?

Later, in Genesis 15, God appeared to Abram in a vision and told him, "Do not be afraid, Abram, I am your shield. Your reward will be very great" (verse 1). What was Abram's response? "Lord God, what can you give me, seeing that I am childless? The heir to my household is Eliezer of Damascus" (verse 2).

Clearly, God's promise to be Abram's shield went right over his head. We soon see Abram going to Egypt (this time Sarai was 90 years old and pregnant) and lying again! He thought he was on his own in dealing with the problems that confronted him. There is no record of his consulting God, requesting His direction, or claiming the promise that had been given him. He didn't understand that the fulfillment of future promises begins with God's guidance and fulfillment of promises today. God showed His patience, love, faithfulness, and generosity as He coached Abram through the process. Leaving his home demonstrated Abram's faith and was counted as righteousness. Belief alone wasn't enough.

> As for me, I trust in your unfailing love; my heart will rejoice when I am brought to safety. I shall sing to the LORD, for he has granted all my desire. (Psalm 13:5–6)

> Keep me, God, for in you have I found refuge. I have said to the LORD, 'You are my Lord; from you alone comes the good I enjoy'....**I shall bless the Lord who has given me counsel: in the night he imparts wisdom to my inmost being**. I have set the Lord before me at all times: with him at my right hand I cannot be shaken. Therefore my heart is glad and my spirit rejoices, my body too rests unafraid....**You will show me the path of life; in your presence is the fullness of joy, at your right hand are pleasures for evermore.** (Psalm 16:1–2, 7–9, 11, emphasis supplied)

Before Sarai became pregnant, she and Abram struggled with God's promise that Abram would have his own son. What did she do when she learned of this promise? She gave her servant Hagar to Abram as a concubine. After all, Sarai was 90 years old; God must not have meant the promise literally. She had already accepted the "reality" that, after all these years, she was not going to have children.

When she overheard a visitor telling Abram that she would have a child, she laughed to herself. And when she heard the visitor ask Abram why she was laughing, she was shocked and frightened. So she lied, denying that she laughed. The visitor's response was simple: "Is anything impossible for the Lord?" (verse 14).

You'd have to agree that Sarai's response was normal. We might even call it practical! Yet her practicality was really distrust. It brought years of grief to their household. Just knowing about God wasn't enough. Their faith had to be exercised.

God's in the business of teaching us that He *can* be trusted and that He is all-powerful. All His counsel is given for our best interest. He wants to be involved in *every* aspect of our lives. He has something fantastic in store for us.

Satan is in the business of placing challenges before us and then encouraging us to think God is not interested in them. For those of us who believe in God, Satan would have us believe God created the earth, set His natural laws in motion, and stepped back to let things take their due course. God's not into meddling, he would say! Satan also adds another twist: God's focus is not on our happiness, but in developing our character. So suck it up, accept your challenges, and use that brain God gave you to make the best of the situation. You can ask for God's help, but don't expect it. Only when you get to heaven will things be perfect. This is the lie Satan feeds us.

When we buy into Satan's lies, we fall into one—or all—of the following traps:

1. We don't think about consulting God
2. We doubt He really loves us
3. We doubt that His intentions are for our benefit
4. We doubt that His promises are for us to use

If you're thinking these lies are too obvious, I'll demonstrate how insidiously Satan works. I can't count the number of times I've heard the following as part of a conversion story: The person was either in a dangerous situation or his life had hit rock bottom. In desperation, he cried out to God, "If you'll save me, I promise I'll serve you for the rest of my life." The inference is that the person was finally willing to sacrifice happiness and serve God because it was his last option.

If you're thinking, "Look, I've got real problems and I'm barely making ends meet; how does any of this help me with my immediate problems?" Well, I've got news for you. This is the exact lesson God tried to teach Israel, and their response was the same. In Moses' last remarks to Israel, he reminds them of God's intentions in adversity, and of His deliverance.

Remember the whole way by which the LORD your God has led you these forty years in the wilderness to humble and test you, and to discover whether or not it was in your heart to keep his commandments. So he afflicted you with hunger and then fed you on manna which neither you nor your fathers had known before, to teach you that **people cannot live on bread alone, but that they live on every word that comes from the mouth of the LORD.** The clothes on your backs did not wear out, nor did your feet blister, all these forty years. Take to heart this lesson: that the LORD your God was disciplining you as a father disciplines his son....He fed you in the wilderness with manna which your fathers had never known, to humble and test you, and **in the end to make you prosper**. (Deuteronomy 8:2–5, 16, emphasis supplied)

Many years later, when Satan tempted Christ in the wilderness, Jesus quoted these same words that Moses had spoken. He also set the record straight by telling us just what our value is in God's eyes.

Are not five sparrows sold for two pence? Yet not one of them is overlooked by God. More than that, even the hairs of your head have all been counted. **Do not be afraid; you are worth more than any number of sparrows** (Luke 12:6–7, emphasis supplied).

Can anxious thought add a day to your life? … Do not set your minds on what you are to eat or drink; do not be anxious....No, **set your minds on his kingdom, and the rest will come to you as well** (Luke 12:25, 29, 31, emphasis supplied).

Whether God should be trusted or not is the focus of the battle between God and Satan. Satan uses any means he can to keep us from understanding and *knowing* by experience that God is *always* faithful and that *it is in our best interest* to trust Him.

Satan wants us to stick God with any of the following adjectives: severe, arbitrary, disinterested, wrathful, or inconsistent. Unfortunately, too many "Christians" have bought Satan's bag of goods. It's no wonder so many churches are struggling. Until we can embrace God's awesome intentions for our lives, faith is impossible! We can say we believe Him, but it will be glaringly apparent that our faith is cultural; we are just going through the motions since it's the acceptable thing to do.

All too often our motives for being Christians are selfish. We just want to either go to heaven or avoid going to hell. We've not seen what God has done so we really can't love Him. *Until we take this first step, it is impossible to harness the power of Christ's death and resurrection to protect us, heal us, and transform us in unimaginable ways.*

Let's review a few Scriptures that emphasize God's faithfulness and love for us.

> **Blessed is anyone who trusts in the LORD, and rests His confidence on him**. He will be like a tree planted by the waterside, that sends out its roots along a stream. When the heat comes it has nothing to fear; its foliage stays green. Without care in a year of drought, it does not fail to bear fruit." (Jeremiah 17:7–8, emphasis supplied)

> **Commit your fortunes to the LORD, and he will sustain you**; he will never let the righteous be shaken." (Psalm 55:22, emphasis supplied)

> God, **I call upon you, for you will answer me**. Bend down your ear to me, listen to my words. Show me how marvelous is your unfailing love: your right hand saves those who seek sanctuary from their assailants. (Psalm 17:6, emphasis supplied)

It's our lack of faith that prevents God from doing what He wants to do. He can't act alone! As long as we keep taking things into our own hands, we keep messing it up; we block what He wants to do and can be trusted to do.

> And **he was unable to do any miracle** there, except that he put his hands on a few sick people and healed them; and he was astonished at their want of faith. (Mark 6:5–6, emphasis supplied)

> There were indeed many widows in Israel in Elijah's time,
> when for three and a half years the skies never opened,
> and famine lay hard over the whole country; yet it was
> to none of these that Elijah was sent, but to a widow at
> Sarepta in the territory of Sidon.(Luke 4:25–26)

On Christmas day, children have no doubt that there will be gifts
to open. They just know! They are in hopeful anticipation, waiting to
open their gifts. This same attitude is what God wants in our lives—a
spirit of hopeful, joyful anticipation!

Once we know that God's purposes are for our good, once we
know He can be trusted and is there to guide and direct us each step of
our lives, we'll move into a new space. We'll see that we're the problem.
We're preventing Him from fulfilling His dream for our lives. It's a
dream we would choose if we had God's vision for our potential.

David says: "I praise you, for you fill me with awe; wonderful you
are, and wonderful your works. You know me through and through"
(Psalm 139:14). We each have a unique combination of talents. We
may not even be aware of the gifts we've been given. I remember
that, as a child, math was my poorest subject. However, years later
when I took finance in graduate school, my professor asked if I'd ever
considered pursuing a teaching career in finance. The thought had
never crossed my mind. Later as an operations manager, I was asked to
create budgets. I learned I had a talent for developing the underlying
assumptions necessary for creating performance-based budgets and
financial forecasting, and was told that few people have these skills.
This wasn't taught; the discovery was accidental. I never viewed myself
as analytical, but subsequent opportunities brought the talent to light.
Nevertheless, God knew and guided my life accordingly.

Unfortunately, our life spans are too short. There's so much God
would like to develop in each of us. The longer we take to involve Him,
the more opportunities we'll miss. Consider the implications. When we
understand this, we'll teach our youth that the later in life they begin
trusting God, the greater the number of awesome opportunities they'll
lose forever. Yes, God takes us where we are, but He had so much more
in store for us if we'd only trusted Him earlier.

Understanding this will help us overcome the fear that we are
somehow sacrificing the "good life" by committing our lives to God.

Nothing could be further from the truth! This is one of the few decisions that we can make in which there is *no* downside risk. Absolutely none! As a matter of fact, we really cannot sacrifice for God; it's all upside.

> God never leads His children otherwise than they would choose to be led, if they could see the end from the beginning and discern the glory of the purpose which they are fulfilling as co-workers with Him. (E.G. White, *Ministry of Healing*, p. 479)

> I speak God's hidden wisdom, his secret purpose framed from the very beginning to bring us to our destined glory....Scripture speaks of 'things beyond our seeing, things beyond our hearing, things beyond our imagining, all prepared by God for those who love him.' (1 Corinthians 2:7, 9)

God wants us to experience and know this firsthand in our lives. Man's history has been a continual struggle to understand this seemingly simple concept. Grasping this and making it our own **is** salvation. God's grace through the power of Jesus' sacrifice and resurrection is what creates our lifelong transformation. This is why salvation begins today and not someday in the future. We all are carrying baggage that is preventing us from enjoying the abundant life. God uses life's events to point out sins that are preventing us from receiving His blessings. He wants us to see our need and experience liberation. This process never stops. This is why it's so urgent we take action today: so we can begin experiencing the joy and the potential that God intended for each of us. God is waiting to walk with you and transform you in a way that you can't even imagine. This **is** the gospel message. "Taste and see that the Lord is good.... They who look to him are radiant with joy; they will never be put out of countenance" (Psalm 34:8,5).

As I write this I am still officially unemployed. I have been using the time to develop a financial tool that will help people manage their money. I don't know what the next steps will bring. My nerves are frequently still on edge. I combat my feelings of apprehension by telling God how I feel, remembering what He's done in the past, repeating His promises, and asking Him, by His grace, to remove my natural feelings of distrust and fear. I've learned that it's my nature to be fearful. It's just what I do. God's promises have become very real and have taken on new relevance. He's answered my prayer! He's promised to provide me with wisdom, discernment, and guidance on an incredible path .

Two of my favorite promises are found in Psalms and Jeremiah:

> When the righteous cry for help, **the LORD hears and sets them free from all their troubles**. The LORD is close to those whose courage is broken; he saves those whose spirit is crushed. Though the misfortunes of one who is righteous be many, the LORD delivers him out of them all (Psalm 34:17–19, emphasis supplied).

> Blessed is anyone who trusts in the LORD, and rests his confidence on him. He will be like a tree planted by the waterside, that sends out its roots along a stream. When the heat comes **it has nothing to fear**; its foliage stays green. **Without care in a year of drought, it does not fail to bear fruit** (Jeremiah 17:7–8, emphasis supplied).

My story isn't finished. I'm still learning to trust. I'm struggling with waiting for the Lord. Sometimes doing nothing is more difficult than doing something. The promise is given by Isaiah:

> These are the words of the Lord GOD, the Holy One of Israel: In calm detachment lies your safety, your strength in quiet trust....Yet the LORD is waiting to show you his favour, and he yearns to have pity on you; for the LORD is a God of justice. **Happy are all who wait for him!**... The Lord may give you bread of adversity and water of affliction, but he who teaches you will no longer keep himself out of sight, but with your own eyes you will see him. If you stray from the path, whether to right or to left, you will hear a voice from behind you sounding in your ears saying, 'This is the way; follow it.' (Isaiah 30:15, 18, 20–21)

We need to learn that God is attentive to everything, both the big and little things in our lives. He will provide for all our needs. Learning this lesson will make a huge difference.

Here are some of my favorite Scriptures on guidance:

Make your paths known to me, LORD; teach me your ways. Lead me by your faithfulness and teach me, for you are God my savior.(Psalm 25:4–5)

> The Lord is good and upright; therefore he teaches sinners the way they should go. He guides the humble in right conduct, and teaches them His way. (vv. 8–9)

> Whoever, fears the LORD will be shown the path he should choose. He will enjoy lasting prosperity, and his descendants will inherit the land. (vv. 12–13)

What wonderful promises!

God wants each of us to *know* that He sees us with special talents that, if given the opportunity, He'll develop beyond our wildest ideas. With each new awesome experience, our spontaneous response is a song of praise. This is how we bless the Lord. We become living examples that He really does know what He's talking about.

The apostle John foretells the day when those who are victorious over Satan will sing the song of Moses and the song of the Lamb.

> "'Great and marvelous are your deeds, O Lord God, sovereign over all; just and true are your ways, O King of the ages. Who shall not fear you, Lord, and do homage to your name? For you alone are holy. All nations shall come and worship before you, for your just decrees stand revealed'" (Revelation 15:3–4).

Until we begin the journey of trusting God, we are robbing ourselves of a tremendously humbling, powerful, and joyful experience. We're called to begin today to trust, to experience His deliverance, and to begin singing our own personal song of Moses. He has a unique journey in mind for each of us, one that helps Him transform us into His image. As the journey unfolds, it will fill us with awe. This is the most powerful and indisputable testimony we can give. It is the salvation experience that begins today. "Let them give thanks to the LORD for his love and for the marvellous things he has done for mankind. Let them offer sacrifices of thanksgiving and tell of his deeds with joyful shouts" (Psalm 107:21–22).

So far We've learned the following lessons:

1. God has always loved us and continues to love us
2. He cares about *every* aspect of our lives and wants to provide solutions
3. He has no favorites
4. The promises He gave Israel remain in effect and are applicable to us
5. His promises can never fail
6. *All* His counsel is given for one reason: to bless us

All of us need to think about each of these gems. There are so many Scriptures in both the Old and New Testament that make these same points. *Once you believe these truths, your hesitance to trust God will wither away, allowing you to see that trusting God is not a sacrifice, but a positive choice.*

As you begin to trust Him, you'll no longer feel that you are giving up something to put God first. Instead, you'll know you are making the single most positive choice of your life. You'll begin walking with God, creating your own marvelous story of His answers to prayer and guidance in your life.

This is the message that God has consistently tried to communicate. He calls us to come and learn that He is trustworthy. There's nothing to lose; there is no downside risk! How's that for an investment opportunity with phenomenal upside potential? He calls us to live always in His presence. He transforms us and blesses us beyond our wildest imagination.

Action Steps:

1. What worries you the most? Write it down.

2. What would you say if someone were to ask, "How do you know that God loves you?" (Don't use Jesus' death on the cross as an example).

3. What troubles you about the concept of God wanting to do something special in your life to demonstrate His love for you?

4. In the Psalms, find two more promises of God's love for you. Write them down.

5. Follow the instructions given in Deuteronomy 8:2 and write down two events in your life that demonstrate God loves you.

6. Do you view yourself the way God views you? Write down the differences.

Additional Scripture for Study

1. Psalm 18:30–32; 16:2, 5–9, 11; 73:23–25, 28

2. Isaiah 46:4–5; 49:8, 10, 14–16

Chapter 3

God's Promises

Hidden
Gem:

Observe the provisions of this covenant and keep them so that you
may be successful in all you do. (Deuteronomy 29:9)

I have a friend, a former fellow employee, who was also laid off. A
month ago, he was very discouraged about his inability to find work.
He wanted to stay in northern Washington; however, because of his
specialized field, he couldn't see how this would be possible. He was also
disappointed by the obvious lack of integrity in many of the companies
with whom he had interviewed. When we spoke, I encouraged him to
consider operating his own business. I shared the following with him:

> Let it be your ambition to live quietly and attend to
> your own business; and to work with your hands, as we
> told you, so that you may command the respect of those
> outside your own number, and at the same time never be
> in want. (1 Thessalonians 4:11–12)

> Commit your way to the LORD; trust in him, and he will
> act. (Psalm 37:5)

My friend just called to report that two of the companies who interviewed him want to use him as a consultant. Another company has requested that he visit them as a follow-up to the proposal he sent them. All of a sudden, it appears that he'll have more work than he can handle! He'll be able to work right out of his home. I could hear the joy and gratitude in his voice. Do you think he'll keep this to himself? Absolutely not! Will new challenges face him? Of course. The difference is, now he's seen God answer his prayers in a wonderful way, according to the promises in the Bible. He'll never forget this.

Knowing that God loves us is the first step toward trusting God and embracing what He has in store for us. Before we take someone's advice, we ask if their counsel is applicable. With God, there are three questions we ask that are all wrapped up together:

> ➤ Many of the promises were given so long ago. Do they still apply?
> ➤ The promises were directed to Israel. Do they apply to me?
> ➤ What do I have to give up to take advantage of these promises?

As we reviewed in the last chapter, *all* of His counsel is given for our benefit because He loves us. Period! The purpose of God's counsel has always been to ensure that we have a full and abundant life. He *never* gave counsel as a prerequisite to salvation. God's focus, like that of any parent, has always been on moving us into a relationship of trust and giving us counsel that would solve our day-to-day problems.

If Israel had followed His counsel, they would have been the envy of the surrounding nations: a nation without the problems everyone else had—the ultimate evangelistic witness. Imagine a community of functional families with close relationships between spouses and children; a community with a consistently strong and vibrant economy based upon integrity and a spirit of generosity; a safe community with no crime and secure borders that never spends a penny on defense. These are the outcomes God promised.

Let's review a few of these promises.

> I have taught you statutes and laws, as the LORD my God commanded me; see that you keep them when you go into and occupy the land. Observe them carefully, for

thereby you will display your wisdom and understanding to other peoples. When they hear about all these statutes, they will say, **'What a wise and understanding people this great nation is!'** What great nation has a god close at hand as the LORD our God is close to us whenever we call to him? What great nation is there whose statutes and laws are so just, as is **all** this code of laws which I am setting before you today? (Deuteronomy 4:5-8, emphasis supplied)

See that you listen, and do all that I command you, and **then it will go well with you and your children after you forever**; for you will be doing what is good and right in the eyes of the LORD your God. (Deuteronomy 12:28, emphasis supplied)

There are many more verses that make clear God's purpose for giving His commandments. The benefits were both for Israel and us. They were clearly *not given* as a condition for our future salvation. We have missed this important distinction! When Paul tells us that the law does not save man, his point is obvious. Like us, the Jews had forgotten, and Paul was addressing their distorted perspective. God's law was given to enrich our lives *today*. In Moses' closing remarks to Israel, he reminds them,

Take to heart all the warnings which I give you this day: command your children to be careful to observe all the words of this law. For you **they are no empty words; they are your very life**, and **by them you will enjoy long life** in the land which you are to occupy after crossing the Jordan. (Deuteronomy 32:46-47, emphasis supplied)

I've rarely heard this perspective from any pulpit. When I've shared this "hidden gem" with people, many have a hard time accepting it. But why should it seem foreign? As a father, I only want the best for my children. I want to see them prosper and live full, happy, productive lives. Since this is true for me, as imperfect and limited as I am, why would it be any different for our heavenly Father, who is perfect, all-powerful, and full of wisdom? He guarantees our outcome if we'll follow His counsel! Christ makes this point in Matthew 7:9–11:

> Would any of you offer his son a stone when he asks for bread, or a snake when he asks for a fish? If you, bad as you are, know how to give good things to your children, how much more will your heavenly Father give good things to those who ask him!

Psalm 119, the longest chapter in the Bible, is entirely focused on the benefits of God's counsel. I encourage you to read the entire chapter, but let's look at a sampling here.

> Happy are they who obey his instruction, who set their heart on finding him. (v. 2)

> I shall heed your law continually, forever and ever; I walk in freedom wherever I will, because I have studied your precepts. (vv. 44–45)

> Your instruction is my everlasting heritage; it is the joy of my heart. I am resolved to fulfill your statutes; they are a reward that never fails. (vv. 111–112)

> Make my step firm according to your promise, and let no wrong have the mastery over me. (v. 133)

> Peace is the reward of those who love your law; no pitfalls beset their path. (v. 165)

David shared that God kept His promise, even beyond what David ever imagined. He was overwhelmed by God's unfailing love and faithfulness. He was filled with such joy, he was unable to keep it to himself! This was what God intended for each of us.

Happy are all who fear the LORD, who conform to his ways. You will enjoy the fruit of your labours, you will be happy and prosperous." (Psalm 128:1–2)

> LORD my God, great things you have done; **your wonders and your purposes are for our good; none can compare with you. I would proclaim them and**

speak of them, but they are more than I can tell.
(Psalm 40:5, emphasis supplied)

If these verses are not clear enough, we have the most direct statement of all given by the angel to Mary in Luke 1:37:**"God's promises can never fail."** How's that for clarity? You'll find that some Bible translations differ a bit. For example, the New King James says, "For with God nothing will be impossible." The intended message is the same: we can count on God to keep His word. The angel was telling Mary that her relative, Elizabeth, who had been unable to conceive, was now six months pregnant. Zacharias doubted the Lord's promise; however, because of our God's power, nothing is impossible. You'll see similar words used in the following four scriptures. Each is in response to individuals doubting that God's promise would come true.

1. "Is anything impossible for the Lord?" (Genesis 18:14). Speaking to Abraham, the Lord emphasized that, despite Sarai's laughing at the idea, she would have a son within a year.

2. In response to Moses' frustration regarding God's promise of one month's supply of meat for the whole nation of Israel, God says, "'Is there a limit to the power of the Lord? You will now see whether or not my words come true.'" (Numbers 11:23)

3. God promises to return to Zion and dwell in Jerusalem. He says, "Even if this may seem impossible to the remnant of this nation in those days, will it also seem impossible to me?" (Zechariah 8:6)

4. Christ reassures his hearers by telling them, "What is impossible for men is possible for God." (Luke 18:27)

David testified that the promises given Israel generations earlier had been fulfilled, thereby demonstrating their validity. These same promises ring true for us today. People are people; our problems and ongoing challenges remain the same. Consequently, *God's counsel never gets old or stale.* It's always vibrant! Psalm 119:160 tells us, "All your words are true; all your just laws will stand forever" (NLT). Fortunately, we are told that God never changes and that He has no favorites. In Moses' final comments to Israel, he says in Deuteronomy 7:9,"Know then that the LORD your God is God, the faithful God; with those who love him and keep his commandments **he keeps covenant and faith for a thousand generations"** (emphasis supplied).

Since Israel's exodus from Egypt in 1440 BC—3,450 years ago—there have not been a thousand generations. According to Wikipedia, "A familial generation is defined as the average time between a mother's first offspring and her daughter's first offspring. The generation length is 25.2 years in the United States as of 2007 and 27.4 years in the United Kingdom as of 2004." If we apply this verse literally, it means that God will keep his covenant and keep faith with us for a total of 25,000 years! God's point is that His promises to Israel are applicable for as long as time lasts. After all, why should a good thing ever end?

David acknowledges this same promise when he expresses thanksgiving and praise over God's protection.

> Look to the Lord and be strong; at all times seek his presence....He is ever mindful of his covenant, the promise he ordained for **a thousand generations**, the covenant made with Abraham, his oath given to Isaac, and confirmed as a statute for Jacob, as **an everlasting covenant** for Israel. (1 Chronicles 16:11, 15–17,emphasis supplied)

Now let's look at some verses that assure us God doesn't change and that the promises He made to Israel also apply to those not of Jewish heritage.

> **God has no favourites.** (Romans 2:11,emphasis supplied)

> **Jesus Christ is the same yesterday, today, and forever**. (Hebrews 13:8,emphasis supplied)

> I am making this covenant, with its oath, not only with you. (Deuteronomy 29:14, NIV).

> **I, the Lord, do not change**, and you have not ceased to be children of Jacob. (Malachi 3:6,emphasis supplied)

> It is the children born through God's promise who are reckoned as Abraham's descendants. (Romans 9:8)

It is those who have faith who are Abraham's sons.
(Galatians 3:7)

After being slaves for two hundred years, the Israelites had lost both their knowledge of God and their ability to govern themselves. Consequently, God had to start with the basics. While teaching them how to get along with each other, He implemented the steps necessary to ensure a functional and harmonious society. He had to demonstrate that, not only was He all-powerful, but their lives depended upon His every word. He began the lesson by showing them that He was worthy of their trust. This is the same lesson we need to learn.

Moses reminds them in Deuteronomy 29:5, "I led you for forty years in the wilderness; the clothes on your back did not wear out, nor did your sandals become worn and fall off your feet; you ate no bread and drank no wine or strong drink, in order that you might learn that I am the LORD your God." Israel saw that the Lord had "'carried [them] all the way...as a father carries his son'" (Deuteronomy 1:31).

Everyone who learns to trust God like this has the same experience without exception; they are filled with awe and gratitude because God provides beyond their expectations. It starts now. We don't wait until we go to heaven. When we get a taste of God's goodness, the anticipation of what heaven will be like just grows and grows! David puts it simply:

> I praise you, for **you fill me with awe; wonderful you are, and wonderful your works**. (Psalm 139:14, emphasis supplied)

> **In all his promises the LORD keeps faith, he is unchanging in all his works;** the LORD supports all who stumble and raises all who are bowed down. All raise their eyes to you in hope, and you give them their food when it is due....The LORD is righteous in all his ways, faithful in all he does; the LORD is near to all who call to him, to all who call to him in sincerity. He fulfills the desire of those who fear him; he hears their cry for help and saves them. (Psalm 145:14–15,17–19, emphasis supplied)

Who could say they're not interested in receiving these promises?

Who could say they are no longer relevant today? Who can say they have claimed them as their own and didn't receive the promised blessings? I've never met such a person! The people who object are the ones who have never stepped out in faith, believing and learning by experience that God is faithful. They've never obeyed His counsel with an air of joyful expectation. Instead, they treat God's Word as if it were given to scold them rather than to uplift and bless them. This is nothing new either; look at what the prophet Jeremiah had to say:

> To whom shall I speak, to whom give warning? Who will hear me? Their ears are blocked: they are incapable of listening; **they treat the LORD's word as a reproach; it has no appeal for them**. (Jeremiah 6:10, emphasis supplied)

> You must never again mention 'the burden of the Lord'; for how can his word be a burden to anyone? (Jeremiah 23:36)

When we don't accept someone's counsel, we don't believe it applies to us. We don't trust them. It doesn't mean we don't like them, it just means we're not convinced we'd be better off by doing what they advise. This was the ongoing problem that God encountered with Israel. They didn't trust Him. God equates distrust with evil and wickedness. Look at the following sequence of events in Numbers 14.

➢ "The LORD said to Moses, 'How long will these people reject Me? And how long will they not believe Me, with all the signs which I have performed among them?'" (v. 11 NKJV).

➢ "Because all these men who have seen My glory and the signs which I did in Egypt and in the wilderness, and have put Me to the test now these ten times, and have not heeded My voice, they certainly shall not see the land of which I swore to their fathers, nor shall any of those who rejected Me see it" (v. 22–23 NKJV).

➢ "The LORD said to Moses and Aaron, 'How long must I tolerate the complaints of this wicked community? I have heard the Israelites making complaints against me'" (vv. 26–27).

Notice that God's description of wicked people is entirely different than the usual definition we hear. His description is tied to one type of person: someone who doesn't trust God, doesn't believe He's present, and refuses to follow His counsel. Applying this definition means we've got problems right inside our churches!

When we fail to seek His presence and rejoice over God's blessings, we end up making futile attempts to find our own paths to happiness. It never works. Whether intentional or not, when we fail to see His blessings, we also remove our focus from His counsel. This means our focus switches to searching out other ways of finding happiness. We'll listen to other people's opinions. Suddenly, we've fallen for the "grass is greener on the other side" illusion. Once we open this door, God's counsel seems to be holding us back from doing what we want.

Those who trust God will know His counsel is for their benefit and will welcome His correction. They will cherish His Word. Then God can let loose His transforming power in their lives because they follow His counsel and have a trusting spirit of joyful obedience.

> Truly he loves his people and blesses his holy ones. They sit at his feet and receive his instruction, the law which Moses laid upon us, as a possession for the assembly of Jacob. (Deuteronomy 33:3–4)

When we don't trust in God and believe His promises, we limit His power in our lives. We've been taught that God is all-powerful and yet we rarely see His power working in our lives like it is shown in Scripture. Why the gap? God's promises are so numerous it is hard to remember them all. There is a promise for every circumstance we might face. Yet, few of us have experienced the power of these promises. What's going on?

> And because of their unbelief, he couldn't do any miracles among them except to place his hands on a few sick people and heal them. And he was amazed at their unbelief. (Mark 6:5–6 NLT)

And so he did only a few miracles there because of their unbelief.(Matthew 13:58 NLT)

Jesus Christ, the Son of God, wanted to do miracles, but He couldn't! He longed to do much more. But for those who watched him grow up, for those who knew Him, he couldn't work miracles. This problem wasn't limited to Jesus. Christ says Elijah had the same problem.

Certainly there were many needy widows in Israel in Elijah's time, when the heavens were closed for three and a half years, and hunger stalked the land. Yet Elijah was not sent to any of them. He was sent instead to a foreigner—a widow of Zarephath in the land of Sidon. (Luke 4:25–26 NLT)

When Elijah visited the widow at Zarephath, she and her son were preparing their last meal so they could die. Jesus is implying that other widows in Israel were suffering too. They ate their last meal and they died. Why? Because of their lack of faith. We often look at people in Scripture like Elijah and think they had some special "in" with God. This couldn't be further from the truth.

This story, found in 1 Kings 17, demonstrates how Elijah's faith was tested numerous times. He repeatedly made the same choice: he could be practical and not ask much of God, or he could take God at His word, believing He would keep His promises. The power of this story is that neither Elijah nor the widow was practical. They didn't know about faith being pragmatic. They expected God to deliver and that's what God did. Let's look at a couple of examples.

"And the ravens brought him bread and meat morning and evening, and he drank from the stream" (v. 6).

As scavengers, ravens eat anything. How many of us would accept bread and meat from a raven? I'm surprised that the raven was willing to give Elijah his food. Elijah certainly could have refused to accept it, expecting God to provide something more appropriate.

'Go now to Zarephath, a village of Sidon, and stay there; I have commanded a widow there to feed you.' He went off to Zarephath, and when he reached the entrance to the village, he saw a widow gathering sticks. He called to her, 'Please bring me a little water in a pitcher to drink.' As she went to fetch it, he called after her, 'Bring me, please, a piece of bread as well.' But she answered, 'As the Lord your God lives, I have no food baked, only a handful of flour in a jar and a little oil in a flask. I am just gathering two or three sticks to go and cook it for my son and myself before we die.' (vv. 9-12)

Certainly there was more than one widow in Zarephath! If it had been me, I would have thought, "I've made a mistake; this must not be the right widow. I shouldn't take her last bit of food from her and her son. There are lots of widows like her in Israel. This woman doesn't even seem to know my God."

The widow's willingness to provide Elijah food and water was an act of faith. There's no indication the Lord spoke to her. How many of us would have sacrificed our last morsel of food for a stranger? Some might call this an act of resignation. She was giving up on life. I don't think so. Verse nine says that the Lord commanded the woman to feed Elijah. She may not have recognized the voice that spoke to her but she had two choices. Even though it hardly seemed practical to feed Elijah, she did it anyway.

Lying behind acts of selfishness is the belief that you are on your own. Success is entirely a result of your own effort, and you can't expect anyone to help you. God is not in the picture. When times are bad, your survival is up to your own ingenuity and persistence.

But a selfish spirit opens the door to dishonesty, greed, and intolerance. The old saying, "The end justifies the means" fits with a spirit of selfishness. Unfortunately, some of the most materially blessed are the most selfish. They believe that what they have achieved has been done by their own strength. With this attitude, there's no room for God. How can God intervene? On what basis does He have to act? He's not being asked to do anything. When this attitude prevails, the negative outcome that is expected actually happens. This is why God was unable to help the other widows in Israel.

God strongly objects when we expect nothing from Him. "I will search with lanterns in Jerusalem's darkest corners to punish those who sit contented in their sins, indifferent to the LORD, thinking he will do nothing at all to them" (Zephaniah 1:12 NLT).

In sharp contrast, God promises that when we trust Him in difficult times, He will provide all of our needs.

> Blessed is anyone who trusts in the LORD, and rests his confidence on him. He will be like a tree planted by the waterside, that sends out its roots along a stream. When the heat comes it has nothing to fear; its foliage stays green. Without care in a year of drought, it does not fail to bear fruit. (Jeremiah 17:7–8)

The spirit of generosity is a demonstration of faith. "The LORD's eyes are turned towards those who fear him, towards those who hope for his unfailing love to deliver them from death, and in famine to preserve them alive" (Psalm 33:18–19). Similarly Psalm 37 says, "I have been young and now have grown old, but **never have I seen the righteous forsaken or their children begging bread**. Day in, day out, such a one lends generously, and his children become a blessing" (vv. 25–26, emphasis supplied). Generosity is an acknowledgement that the Lord has provided and will continue to provide for your needs.

> Afterwards the son of the woman, the owner of the house, fell ill and was in a very bad way, until at last his breathing stopped. The woman said to Elijah, 'What made you interfere, you man of God? You came here to bring my sins to light and cause my son's death!' 'Give me your son,' he said. He took the boy from her arms and carried him up to the roof-chamber where his lodging was, and laid him on his bed. He called out to the LORD, 'LORD my God, is this your care for the widow with whom I lodge, that **you have been so cruel** to her son?' Then he breathed deeply on the child three times and called to the LORD, 'I pray, LORD my God, let the breath of life return to the body of this child.' (I Kings 17:17–21, emphasis supplied)

Did Elijah pray for the boy before he died? We aren't told in Scripture. But upon the boy's death, Elijah prays boldly, using strong language—"you have been so cruel." I would have stopped praying then, believing the boy's death was just another example of the terrible effects of sin and that I had done all I could. At that point, I would do my best to comfort the widow.

But Elijah took a different approach. He knew God was a loving God. What he couldn't understand was why it took Him so long to act. In short, Elijah wasn't going to take "no" for an answer! The Lord heard Elijah's prayer. The widow's response demonstrates the reason for God's delay: "She said to Elijah, 'Now I know for certain that you are a man of God and that the word of the LORD on your lips is truth'" (v. 24). It took the healing of her son for the widow to finally be convinced.

God asks us to *know* Him and put our trust in Him, believing He desires to demonstrate His power in the simplest things that concern us. When we exercise our faith by claiming His promises, it frees Him to act. The results will always surprise us, and we will sing His praises. We will be living witnesses of what God has wanted to do in His children's lives from the first day of creation. Israel lost sight of this, and so have we. Consequently, our Christian experience lacks the power of God.

I am convinced that, because our focus has always been on going to heaven, we're not experiencing the abundant life that God intends for us to live today. Our focus on the future and our insistence that faith must be practical has caused us to entirely miss God's central purpose. God wants us to know He is worthy of our trust, and although we live in a sinful world, He's looking out for our best interests. This is the issue in the battle between God and Satan. Pragmatic, sensible faith robs God of His opportunity to demonstrate His love and faithfulness. Pragmatic, practical faith robs us of experiencing an entirely different way of life—God's way. This missing piece of the puzzle goes a long way toward providing the insight we need to boost our faith and rid us of fear and doubt.

In the opening chapter of Genesis, when God created man, He clearly stated that we were created in His image. We don't have to look any further than our homes, families, and daily challenges to know that humanity has fallen far from that image. If looking at your own circumstances isn't enough, pick up a newspaper or watch television. You won't need to watch for very long. This is also why there's such a focus on looking forward to heaven. We all hope for the day when we don't have to put up with all the pain and other stuff that God never intended for us to experience.

Our problem is not that we intentionally doubt the generosity of God's promises. Instead, when things aren't going right, we're sure that God has left us in some kind of holding pattern. We don't expect Him to make things right until we get to heaven. In the meantime, it's up to us to work through our problems. Our preoccupation with coping leaves no room for Him to impact our lives. Nothing could be further from the truth!

Sin entered the picture because of a lack of faith and obedience. God desires for us to experience His blessings. When we fail to trust Him and embrace His guidance it prevents us from being blessed. Sin is anything that prevents us from experiencing the blessings God intends for our lives *today*. Failing to have faith and being disobedient bring the same result: a life that falls short of achieving the blessings He desires. This is what Paul meant when he said, "All alike have sinned, and are deprived of the divine glory" (Romans 3:23). Our heavenly Father and His Son, Jesus Christ, provided a way to free us of the addictive and destructive power of sin and to complete the work that they originally intended. In the following scriptures, Paul affirms God's intention to begin fulfilling His original design *now:*

> [You] have put on the new nature which is **constantly being renewed in the image of its Creator and brought to know God**." (Colossians 3:10, emphasis supplied)

> You must…put on **the new nature created in God's likeness**, which **shows itself in the upright and devout life** called for by the truth. (Ephesians 4:23–24 emphasis supplied)

> Because for us there is no veil over the face, we all see as in a mirror the glory of the Lord, and **we are being transformed into his likeness with ever increasing glory**, through the power of the Lord who is the Spirit. (2 Corinthians 3:18, emphasis supplied)

It was for this that he called you through the gospel we brought, so that **you might come to possess the splendour** of our Lord Jesus Christ." (2 Thessalonians 2:14, emphasis supplied)

In a word, as God's dear children **you must be like him**. (Ephesians 5:1, emphasis supplied)

Isaiah uses a beautiful analogy to reassure us that God's words will fulfill His purpose.

"As the rain and snow come down from the heavens and do not return there without watering the earth, making it produce grain to give seed for sowing and bread to eat, so is it with my word issuing from my mouth; it will not return to me empty without accomplishing my purpose and succeeding in the task for which I sent it" (Isaiah 55:10–11).

These verses demonstrate God's love for us! It is with this in mind that Peter made the following observation:

God's divine power **has bestowed on us everything that makes for life and true religion**, through our knowledge of him who called us by his own glory and goodness. In this way he has given us his promises, great beyond all price, so that through them you may escape the corruption with which lust has infected the world, **and may come to share in the very being of God**. (2 Peter 1:3–4, emphasis supplied)

Understanding God's purpose and commitment puts His promises in a whole new light! Each of His promises can be placed in one of the following categories:
- ➢ Guidance
- ➢ Encouragement, Hope, and Comfort
- ➢ Deliverance, Liberation, and Healing from the terrible effects of disobedience
- ➢ Commitment to meet our needs

Take any promise found in Scripture, and it will fit it into one of these categories. Try it! So, with such a clear purpose, there's really just one question left: Will you believe it? We must begin to take God at His word. Too often, when we read a promise, we automatically think of situations in which it appears the promise didn't come true. Next time you read a promise and you question whether it applies to you, notice how the thought spontaneously jumps into your head. This is Satan speaking to you. Ignore him, and believe that God gave the promise for your current situation. Believe Him! Ask God to take away your doubt. He'll do it!

None of these promises are of any value if we cannot bring ourselves to believe that God's way is the *only* way that brings a happy and joyful life. When will we believe that God knows what He's talking about? It was over this point that Satan first tempted Adam and Eve. He's continued the same assault on us. Satan knows that, when we are unsettled over a question, he's got us just where he wants us. This was the insidious nature behind his comment to Eve in Genesis 3:5, "'God knows that, as soon as you eat it, your eyes will be opened and you will be like God himself, knowing both good and evil.'"

For example, we have all known a teenager who tells his parents he knows what's best for his own life. All of us have gone through that phase ourselves. We, too, questioned our parent's counsel, believing we were smart enough to make the best decisions. This is exactly the same thought process we go through with God. Satan has continued to repeat this same temptation to every successive generation. He knows that God's power is *only* unleashed by our faith, so he focuses on undermining it. It just takes one of the following:

➤ Distorting God's character through people who claim to know Him
➤ Discouraging us through difficult circumstances or self-doubt
➤ Chaining us to addictions *or* building up our ego, both of which prevent us from accurately assessing our situation
➤ Keeping us too busy or distracted so we don't discover the life God has in store for us

When other people's opinions agree with our biases, our nature encourages us to accept their word as fact. We see this dynamic in social circles and in politics. We love to accept innuendo that conveniently fits into our current vision of life. We don't like to admit that we might be wrong. As a matter of fact, if we think we might be wrong, we look for something that will strengthen our defense. We don't want to make the effort to discover the truth, even if it's to our benefit! Our disappointments make us skeptical about believing something that seems too good to be true. Yet, what God desires to do is so simple, and there is no downside!

Fortunately for us, God doesn't require that we have a lot of faith to get started. Jesus said it only takes faith as tiny as a mustard seed. And what will the result be? We'll be able to move a mountain.

> Afterwards the disciples came to Jesus and asked him privately, 'Why could we not drive it out?' He answered, 'Your faith is too small. Truly I tell you: if you have faith no bigger than a mustard seed, you will say to this mountain, "Move from here to there!" and it will move; nothing will be impossible for you.' (Matthew 17:19–20)

How many of us believe that Jesus means what He says? When we understand God's purposes, we can pray with heartfelt faith, claiming the promise that fits our situation.

> My dear friends, **if our conscience does not condemn us**, then **we can approach God with confidence, and obtain from him whatever we ask, because** we are keeping his commands and **doing what he approves**. (1 John 3:21–22, emphasis supplied)

> **We can approach God with this confidence**: if we make requests which accord with his will, he listens to us; and if we know that our requests are heard, **we also know that all we ask of him is ours**. (1 John 5:14–15, emphasis supplied)

The only way God can prove that Satan is a liar is by our individual experiences. They must confirm God's faithfulness and that His ways really are loving and sure. This is how God is vindicated. Theological arguments won't cut it. But personal stories are irrefutable. Our lives are what catch a person's attention, encouraging them to step out of their comfort zone and put fear and doubt aside. Understanding God's commitment and desire to be our partner in life makes all the difference. Once we know God's purpose is to restore, protect, and provide, we can stop wondering if He's present in our lives.

> Yet Jerusalem says, "The LORD has deserted us; the Lord has forgotten us." Never! Can a mother forget her nursing child? Can she feel no love for the child she has borne? But even if that were possible, I would not forget you! See, I have written your name on my hand. (Isaiah 49:14–16 NLT)

> Listen, and I will tell you where to get food that is good for the soul! Come to me with your ears wide open. Listen, for the life of your soul is at stake. I am ready to make an everlasting covenant with you. I will give you all the mercies and unfailing love that I promised to David. (Isaiah 55:2–3 NLT)

> This, says the LORD, is my covenant, which I make with them: My spirit which rests on you and my words which I have put into your mouth will never fail you from generation to generation of your descendants from now on, forevermore. The Lord has said it. (Isaiah 59:21)

What an exciting invitation! He calls us to experience His power. Paul sums it up in 1 Corinthians 4:20: "For the kingdom of God is not a matter of words, but of power."

We have such tremendous examples of people who took God at His word. Are we also willing to believe Him and begin experiencing His power to restore us in His image? If so, take that first small step of faith today!

Make Psalm 25 your prayer. The Holy Spirit will give you confidence and peace.

> LORD my God, to you I lift my heart. In you I trust: do not let me be put to shame, do not let my enemies exult over me. No one whose hope is in you is put to shame; but shame comes to all who break faith without cause.

Make your paths known to me, LORD; teach me your ways. Lead me by your faithfulness and teach me, for you are God my saviour; in you I put my hope all day long.... The Lord is good and upright; therefore he teaches sinners the way they should go. He guides the humble in right conduct, and teaches them his way. All the paths of the LORD are loving and sure to those who keep his covenant and his solemn charge. LORD, for the honour of your name forgive my wickedness, great though it is. Whoever fears the LORD will be shown the path he should choose. He will enjoy lasting prosperity, and his descendants will inherit the land. The LORD confides his purposes to those who fear him; his covenant is for their instruction. My eyes are ever on the LORD, who alone can free my feet from the net. (Psalm 25:1–5, 8–15)

Action Steps

1. What bothers you about the idea that all God's counsel is given for your benefit?

2. Choose your favorite scriptures that reinforce this concept. Write them down.

3. Since God is no respecter of persons, what impact can this concept have on your relationship with God and how you pray?

4. Does the idea that you can limit God's power bother you? If so, write down your reasons.

5. Do you really want God's correction? If not, why not?

6. What impact will joyful obedience have in your life?

7. What changes would you like to make in your life? Write them down and share them with an accountability partner.

Additional Scripture for Study

Psalm 103
Psalm 107:19–22, 35–43
Psalm 109:26–31
Psalm 111

Chapter 4

Taming Our Doubts

Hidden
Gem:

When doubts filled my mind, your comfort gave me renewed hope and cheer. (Psalm 94:19 NLT)

While I was working as Chief Financial Officer of a small hospital on Kauai, the management team faced seemingly insurmountable financial challenges. Approximately two months after I began as CFO, the medical group that supported the hospital failed to meet payroll. Some days we had no more than five or six people hospitalized. It felt like we were deluding ourselves to think we could improve the hospital's financial situation. Words just can't describe the sense of discouragement and futility I frequently felt. Powerful forces within the legislature supported closing the hospital. The hospital system's CEO showed up at the hospital to announce its closure. Yet the community demanded that it remain open.

My strategy for dealing with the crisis was to create a hospital based physician clinic that would enable the hospital to control its own destiny. It took much persuasion to accomplish, but once the hospital began to pursue this strategy, the financial picture did improve. It is now filled with patients.

During this extremely stressful time, I read in Ephesians 5:18–20 that we are to sing songs and give thanks in everything. I wrote out the words of hymns that had special meaning to me and sang them during my daily forty-five-minute commute. I found my spirits lifting. My fellow employees began asking how I was able to be so positive with all the pressure I faced. When I shared my secret with them, a couple took copies of the hymns home for their own use.

Because God is not a respecter of persons, God's promise or covenant to Abraham has been repeated many times, first to Israel and now to us. God wanted Israel to know He was dwelling with them. Because of His love, He called them to stay in His presence, which was as much a pleasure for God as it was vital to Israel's very existence. At first, their need was not obvious to them, but they soon came to understand that abiding in His presence was necessary for their protection, guidance, and on-going development. We, too, have failed to understand the urgency of remaining in God's presence.

We see God teaching Israel that "Man does not live on bread alone but on every word that comes from the mouth of the LORD" (Deuteronomy 8:3 NIV) In our focus on the future, we've missed the importance of dwelling in His presence *today*. God repeats this idea to Israel in Exodus 29:45–46. "I will live among the people of Israel and be their God, and they will know that I am the LORD their God. I am the one who brought them out of Egypt so that I could live among them. I am the LORD their God" (NLT).

In Exodus 17:7, when Israel began complaining for lack of water, God called the place "Massah and Meribah, because the Israelites had disputed with him and put the LORD to the test with their question, '**is the LORD in our midst or not**?'" (emphasis supplied)

It wasn't enough for God to deliver Israel from Egypt, to visibly lead them with a pillar of cloud by day and fire by night, or give them clothes that didn't wear out, manna to eat, and water to drink. He commands Moses to "Make me a sanctuary, and **I shall dwell among** the Israelites" (Exodus 25:8).

God wanted them to know firsthand that He was there to deliver, protect, guide, and provide for them—just like any good parent. He wanted them to see the results of their special partnership. By calling upon His name, they were to *know* their success was by His hand and not theirs. Moses told them, "He is your proud boast, your God who has done for you these great and terrible things which you saw for yourselves" (Deuteronomy 10:21).

When Israel quickly forgot the promises given to them by God, Moses *demands that God be in their presence,* and God complies. Moses prays,

> 'If I have indeed won your favour, then **teach me to know your ways**, so that I can know and continue in favour with you, for this nation is your own people.'The LORD answered, '**I shall go myself and set your mind at rest**.' Moses said to him, 'Indeed if you do not go yourself, do not send us up from here; for how can it ever be known that I and your people have found favour with you, except by your going with us? So **we shall be distinct**, I and your people, from all the peoples on earth.' The LORD said to Moses, 'I shall do what you have asked, because **you have found favour with me, and I know you by name**.' (Exodus 33:13–17,emphasis supplied)

When King Solomon allowed his foreign wives to turn him away from the Lord, the Lord gave the same promise to Jeroboam, Solomon's assistant.

> If you pay heed to all my commands, if you conform to my ways and do what is right in my eyes, observing my statutes and commandments as my servant David did, **then I shall be with you**. I shall establish your family forever as I did for David; I shall give Israel to you. (1 Kings 11:38, emphasis supplied)

God fulfilled the prophecy and made Jeroboam king over Israel, but, tragically, Jeroboam couldn't bring himself to trust God. God's dream for him seemed too good to be true. Jeroboam feared that, if the ten tribes of Israel continued to return to Jerusalem to worship God, he would lose their allegiance. Consequently, he created his own solution and reestablished the worship of golden calves. This brought about the moral decay and eventual scattering of the ten tribes of Israel. Furthermore, the two tribes of Judah followed Jeroboam's example and came to the same end. Because King Jeroboam couldn't bring himself to believe that God could be trusted, he missed out on an experience of a lifetime. His successors all followed the same dangerous path of distrust.

Notice, it was a lack of trust—a failure to believe that God had something fabulous in store—that caused the problem. Creating the golden calves was the effect. We make the same mistake.

Isaiah foretells that the coming Messiah is to be given the name Emmanuel, meaning "God with us" (Isaiah 7:14). This name was meant to fill the people's hearts with hope. Jesus' earthly father, Joseph, is told in a dream, "'A virgin will conceive and bear a son, and he shall be called Emmanuel,' a name which means 'God is with us'" (Matthew 1:23). Jesus repeats the promise just before he is crucified.

> 'If you dwell in me, and my words dwell in you, ask whatever you want, and you shall have it. This is how my Father is glorified: you are to bear fruit in plenty and so be my disciples. **As the Father has loved me, so I have loved** you. **Dwell in my love**. If you heed my commands, you will dwell in my love, as I have heeded my Father's commands and dwell in his love. **I have spoken thus to you so that my joy may be in you, and your joy complete**.' (John 15:7–11, emphasis supplied)

Reframing our attitudes from "can'ts" or "shouldn'ts" to one of positive choices sounds too simple. Knowing that each positive choice we make is opening a door to another blessing creates a new frame of reference. This new attitude creates a desire to learn more, since ignorance means we're missing out on a blessing God intends for us.

Unfortunately, this is a problem that God has consistently struggled to beat. We repeatedly see people misinterpreting the counsel He provides as either a limitation or a sacrifice that keeps them from enjoying life. There are two examples worth considering.

The book of Deuteronomy is Moses' final remarks before he dies. In it, he reviews God's tremendous love for Israel, God's promises, the laws given to protect and enrich their lives, and Israel's past failures. Then he warns them that their continued failure to trust God will bring a disastrous future. He gives this key warning in Deuteronomy 28:47: "You have not served the LORD your God, rejoicing in gladness of heart over all your blessings." He reminds them that complaining is distrusting God—doubting God's presence and that He is working to turn even the worst of situations into positive outcomes.

Near the end of Moses' remarks, he characterizes what God has done for Israel: "Truly he loves his people and blesses his holy ones. They sit at his feet and receive his instruction, the law which Moses laid upon us, as a possession for the assembly of Jacob" (Deuteronomy 33:3–4).

Clearly, God's law was given to bless and bring prosperity. It's important to remember that Moses never says God gave these words as a condition for salvation. Present and future salvation comes only by trusting God day by day, accepting His guidance, and following His counsel. Salvation is about believing He knows what He's talking about. The law was given as a blessing for their lives in the present.

God has a long history of advising us to focus on today. He takes care of tomorrow! Moses writes:

> Take to heart all the warnings which I give you this day: command your children to be careful to observe all the words of this law. For you they are no empty words; **they are your very life, and by them you will enjoy long life in the land which you are to occupy after crossing the Jordan**. (Deuteronomy 32:46–47, emphasis supplied)

Compare this with Psalm 119, which contains 176 verses. Can you guess what it's about? The joys and blessings associated with God's law! As David says in another Psalm,

> The law of the LORD is perfect and **revives the soul**. The LORD's instruction never fails; it **makes the simple wise**. The precepts of the LORD are right and **give joy to the heart**. The commandment of the LORD is pure and **gives light to the eyes**. (Psalm 19:7–8, emphasis supplied)

These are active verbs, life-transforming experiences meant for us now. Who wouldn't want them?

When King David brought the Ark of the Covenant back to Jerusalem, he sang a song of thanksgiving to the Lord: "Exult in his holy name; O worshipers of the LORD, rejoice! Search for the LORD and for his strength, and keep on searching" (1 Chronicles 16:10–11 NLT).

For some of you, this seems totally at odds with what you've been taught all your lives regarding the law given to Moses. If all God's ways are loving and sure, our salvation can't depend upon which side of the cross we were born. If there were a difference, we would struggle with the following questions:

➤ How would this be fair to the person who lived and died before Jesus' death and resurrection?

➤ How could we be absolutely sure that God acts in our best interest?

➤ This would mean that God loves those born after Christ's death more than those born before His death. How could we be sure that God loves each of us equally?

When the case is made that the law was done away with at the cross, it leaves nagging doubts that will keep us from trusting God with all our heart. When there are doubts, God's power will be absent. Without His power, we can't be transformed into His image. Instead of faith being an active demonstration of His might, it becomes a lifeless ritual without relevance. If we accept this line of reasoning, we're saying that all God's ways are *not* loving and sure. When we don't believe this, the door is open for us to entertain a wide range of distorted views that are not supported by Scripture.

See how one seemingly small distortion can be so undermining?

Don't think this response is anything new. Nagging doubts are an old problem. In Moses' final remarks to Israel in Deuteronomy, he repeats the same promise given to Abraham, Isaac, and Jacob twenty times. You don't need to repeat something twenty times if everybody already gets it! And you know what? We still don't get it!

Unfortunately, most people don't even know about these promises; if they do, they don't realize they're found in Deuteronomy. Many other books of the Bible reference Deuteronomy including Joshua, Judges, 1 Chronicles, Isaiah, Jeremiah, Ezekiel, Daniel, Zephaniah, Malachi, Matthew, Mark, Luke, John, Romans, and Hebrews. Yet the book of Deuteronomy is misinterpreted as no longer relevant. Nothing could be further from the truth!

Promises are great. But when we're facing problems, it's hard for us to believe that God means what He says. What steps can we take so the reality of the promise is greater than our problem?

> **Be of good courage**, and **He shall strengthen your heart,** all you who hope in the LORD. (Psalm 31:24 NKJV, emphasis supplied)

> **Wait** on the LORD; **be of good courage**, and **He shall strengthen your heart**; Wait, I say, on the LORD! (Psalm 27:14 NKJV, emphasis supplied)

Both verses ask us to have courage, which is the ability to do something that frightens us or the spirit that enables us to face difficulty, danger, or pain without fear. Courage is required to put into action the steps to achieve our desired outcome. This is why real faith is hard and is rarely seen. Instead of faith, we usually give lip service to what we *want* to believe. But belief is demonstrated by action! Both of these verses command us to wait and be confident that God *will* act. When we make this choice, He promises to strengthen our hearts. The promise comes with a condition; we have a part to play.

These are some awesome promises. But while they uplift my spirits when I read them, feelings of thankfulness and peace don't always follow me when things are going wrong. Instead, when circumstances beyond my control lead to unpleasant outcomes, I begin to anticipate worst-case scenarios.

In short, while my head may remember these great promises, my heart just doesn't go along. Some people are naturally wired to be positive, but not me! As a matter of fact, I begin to focus on the seemingly inevitable bad outcome, even though my worst fears rarely, if ever, come true. I find myself thinking that I'm in this all by myself.

The good news is that, over time, my attitude has changed. I've become more positive. How do I know? It's not because I feel any different, but because my family, friends, and business associates have made this observation. To me, I'm still struggling like I always have.

How do we get our hearts to accept that the promises are for our use? This is hardly a unique problem. It's at the very core of developing a trusting relationship with God. What should we expect of Him? Or, as a friend recently asked, "What's realistic?"

We need to banish the idea of realistic expectations from our thoughts. There is no way of determining what's realistic to God. Our expectations reflect what *we've* accepted as limitations. When we ask what's realistic, we're expressing our belief that God will not intervene, that He's merely passively involved.

God won't disappoint those with this mindset. For example, He promises to give wisdom freely to anyone who asks, but He also gives a condition:

> But when you ask him, be sure that you really expect him to answer, for a doubtful mind is as unsettled as a wave of the sea that is driven and tossed by the wind. People like that should not expect to receive anything from the Lord. They can't make up their minds. They waver back and forth in everything they do. (James 1:6–8 NLT)

If you ask for wisdom to make a sound decision, *know* that God will give you the answer. There's nothing left to wonder about. He's clearly promised to give you wisdom if you ask for it. If you do wonder, your prayer won't be answered. There's no room for asking if it's realistic to expect God to provide the wisdom to make a wise decision. Pondering it means you've already decided not to expect an answer. You're not going to wait; you're not going to allow Him to strengthen your heart. You've decided once again to go it alone.

One of the most graphic illustrations of this is found in Exodus 17:1–7. Moses, David, and Paul later refer to this unfortunate sequence of events. It's a lesson that we are not to repeat.

> The whole community of Israel set out from the wilderness of Sin and traveled by stages **as the Lord directed**. They encamped at Rephidim, but there was no water for the people to drink and a dispute arose between them and Moses. When they said, 'Give us water to drink,' Moses said, 'Why do you dispute with me? **Why do you challenge the Lord?**' The people became so thirsty there that they raised an outcry against Moses: 'Why have you brought us out of Egypt with our children and our herds to let us die of thirst?' Moses appealed to the Lord,

'What shall I do with these people? In a moment they will be stoning me.' The LORD answered, 'Go forward ahead of the people; take with you some of the elders of Israel and bring along the staff with which you struck the Nile. Go, you will find me waiting for you there, by a rock in Horeb. Strike the rock; water will pour out of it for the people to drink.' Moses did this in the sight of the elders of Israel. He named the place Massah and Meribah, because **the Israelites had disputed with him and put the LORD to the test with their question, 'Is the Lord in our midst or not?'** (emphasis supplied)

Wouldn't we all have complained? After all, water is one of the most basic needs for life. Just picture two million people walking across the hot Sinai desert without water. After witnessing the great things God had done for them, they were probably expecting a miracle, but when none came, the past no longer mattered. The future promise didn't matter, either. It was all about the present. What good is a land flowing with milk and honey if you're dead?

Little did they know their distrust would bring them exactly the outcome they feared most. They would never see the land promised them.

What should they have realistically expected? Certainly not water gushing from a rock! Yet, look at Moses' reaction. First, he never complained, even though he was thirsty too. Second, he saw this as Israel questioning God's promise to go with them and provide for their needs. They were to ask, wait on God to provide, and continue walking, believing that God would do as He promised.

Just because God had delivered them in the past didn't mean life would be free of challenges. They had expectations for how things should be done. When God didn't meet them, they assumed He was not present. They would have done much better if they had no expectations—if they had taken one day at a time without projecting realistic outcomes onto their current situation.

Trusting God means not accepting the apparent reality of a situation; it means not defining "realistic" outcomes. We need to stop acting as if we're prophets. We don't have the full picture, and neither does Satan.

The story is told of the King of Aram sending a strong force of horses and chariots to seize Elisha. When Elisha's assistant stepped outside the next morning and told the prophet what he saw,

> Elisha answered, 'Do not be afraid, for those on our side are more than those on theirs.' He offered this prayer: 'LORD, open his eyes and let him see.' The LORD opened the young man's eyes, and he saw the hills covered with horses and chariots of fire all around Elisha. (2 Kings 6:16–17)

Instead of pondering "realistic" expectations, stop and remember God's promises, praise Him, and ask for His intervention. Then wait, watching for His response. When you receive it, praise Him again for His answer. Notice, however, that we should even praise Him before we see His response!

Most of us don't even get to Step One; we don't stop and remember what He's done in the past. We simply assume that the problem we're experiencing is ours to deal with. We don't stop to consider it as an opportunity for a loving Father to demonstrate that He can use the "junk" in our lives to prove that He is in control.

The following steps have helped me keep my head in the right place during difficult times:

1. Find Your Special Promise
2. Learn the Difference between God's Voice and Satan's Voice
3. Remember God's Previous Answers
4. Acknowledge Your Feelings
5. Remember: God's Purpose is to Heal
6. Take Care of Yourself
7. Sing Songs of Gratitude to Lift Your Spirit
8. Share What God is Teaching You
9. Keep Repeating This Process

Let's consider each of these steps in more detail.

Find Your Special Promise

We've already touched on so many wonderful promises. Take one or two of them, write them down, review them daily, and make them a part of your prayers. Here are some of my favorites:

> 'God's promises can never fail.' (Luke 1:37)

> Blessed is anyone who trusts in the LORD, and rests his confidence on him. He will be like a tree planted by the waterside, that sends out its roots along a stream. When the heat comes it has nothing to fear; its foliage stays green. Without care in a year of drought, it does not fail to bear fruit. (Jeremiah 17:7–8)

> Put all your trust in the LORD and do not rely on your own understanding. At every step you take keep him in mind, and he will direct your path. (Proverbs 3:5–6)

Learn the Difference Between God's Voice and Satan's Voice

As a kid, I loved watching cartoons (actually, I still do!). My favorites were Bugs Bunny, Daffy Duck, and the Road Runner. I remember scenes where an angel sat on one shoulder talking into the character's ear, while Satan sat on the other shoulder.

While this depiction made me laugh, it's not far from the truth. The different voices are fairly easy to distinguish. In either case, their presence is marked by a sudden thought that pops up from nowhere. God's voice provides direction, encouragement, or a warning to prevent harm. His message is entirely consistent with the promises given in Scripture, and His purpose is always to uplift us and to develop our unique talents. On the other hand, Satan's voice encourages us to be critical of ourselves or others, to do what we know will harm us, to discourage us from taking seemingly "unreasonable" risks, or to justify vengeful actions.

In the first fourteen months after we moved to Washington, I was offered several attractive job opportunities back in Hawaii, each allowing me to earn significantly more money than I had before leaving. With each offer, I heard two distinct voices. One promised that if I stay the course, my family would be blessed. The other voice reminded me of all the problems: our parents had been opposed to our move; I had no job, no connections, and no family support structure; our decision to move here had put the family at risk. How could that be God's will? I'd gotten it all wrong! In short, this voice said I should get my act together, repair the damage, and return home.

Needless to say, we stayed, and we received the blessings we'd hoped for. Our children, who have grown up in a spiritually healthier community, have learned the joy of service and developed positive friendships that have encouraged them to make the right life decisions. Furthermore, other doors have opened, giving new life to dreams that, I thought, had died long ago. The verse in Hebrews 11:15 became very personal to me: "If their thoughts had been with the country they had left, they could have found opportunity to return." Other passages also took on new meaning, such as these:

> **Be on the alert! Wake up**! Your enemy the devil, like a roaring lion, prowls around **looking for someone to devour**. Stand up to him, firm in your faith, and remember that your fellow-Christians in this world are going through the same kinds of suffering. (1 Peter 5:8–9, emphasis supplied)

> Finally, find your strength in the Lord, in his mighty power. Put on the full armour provided by God, so that you may be able to stand firm against the stratagems of the devil. For our struggle is not against human foes but against cosmic powers, against the authorities and potentates of this dark age, against the superhuman forces of evil in the heavenly realms. (Ephesians 6:10–12)

We need to acknowledge that our struggles aren't simply with ourselves and those around us. The sooner we are willing to make this part of our day-to-day thinking, the sooner God's promises will have greater power. We'll feel a greater need for prayer, our prayers will take on added urgency, and we'll see more concrete and tangible answers.

Christ assures us of our ability to know God's voice:

He who enters by the door is the shepherd in charge of the sheep. The door keeper admits him, and the sheep hear his voice; he calls his own sheep by name, and leads them out. When he has brought them all out, he goes ahead of them and the sheep follow, because they know his voice....I am the good shepherd; I know my own and my own know me, as the Father knows me and I know the Father; and I lay down my life for the sheep. But there are other sheep of mine, not belonging to this fold; I must lead them as well, and **they too will listen to my voice**. There will then be one flock, one shepherd. (John 10:2–4, 14–16, emphasis added)

Remember God's Previous Answers

When events in my life look dark, I begin to wonder if I've made a mistake and should retrace my steps. This is the time when I need to remember the past answers to prayer that have brought me to this place. In doing so, I realize I'm not alone. Psalm 78:6–7 reminds me,

So that it might be known to a future generation, to children yet to be born, and they in turn would repeat it to their children. They were charged **to put their trust in God, to hold his great acts ever in mind** and to keep his commandments. (emphasis added)

As I continue to find my footing in a new community in economically challenging times, I go back and review the doors that have opened; making it absolutely clear which path I should take. These past answers *force* me to reject any suspicion that I arrived here by luck. It simply isn't possible. When I also look at the results of taking this path—the health of my children—I am overcome with a sense of gratitude, awe, and joy for the Lord's faithfulness.

During difficult times, I also reread Bible stories such as those in Exodus 17 (Israel complaining about not having water) and Genesis 12 (Abraham leaving his home without knowing where he was going). These chapters reaffirm what I must do in spite of my fear and apprehension.

Acknowledge Your Feelings

Let's face it—our emotions play a larger-than-life role in determining our actions. That's why reviewing what God has done in our past, as well as in the lives of others, is so important. It tips the balance toward acting from what we know to be true rather than acting from how we feel. However, many times the fear is still there. So, acknowledge how you feel. It's a reflection of who you are. Don't beat yourself up! Once again, start with a promise:

> I wish you joy in the Lord always. Again I say: all joy be yours. Be known to everyone for your consideration of others. The Lord is near; **do not be anxious, but in everything make your requests known to God in prayer and petition with thanksgiving**. Then **the peace of God** which is beyond all understanding, **will guard your hearts and your thoughts in Christ Jesus**. (Philippians 4:4–7, emphasis added)

Claim the promise, believing that God is with you. Along with your request for direction, acknowledge your fear and claim His promise of peace. God knows that we can't see tomorrow, but He's promised to provide all we need to face our challenges.

Remember God's Purpose is to Heal

God's healing *is* the power of the gospel in both the Old and New Testament. It's the center of the sanctuary service and the purpose of Christ's death on the cross. It's the reality of the power of God's grace. God takes no pleasure in accepting us, forgiving us, and then leaving us as He found us. That's not a picture of a loving God. Fear and discouragement are paralyzing, but peace brings clarity and assurance, which contribute to our enjoyment of life. Consequently, God's promise to provide healing and peace is a necessity that also brings relevance to the gospel.

Heal me, Lord, and I shall be healed, save me and I shall be saved; for you are my praise. (Jeremiah 17:14)

The spirit of the Lord God is upon me because the Lord

has anointed me; he has sent me to announce good news to the humble, to bind up the broken-hearted, to proclaim liberty to captives, release to those in prison; to proclaim a year of the Lord's favour and a day of the vengeance of our God; to comfort all who mourn, to give them garlands instead of ashes, oil of gladness instead of mourners' tears, a garment of splendour for the heavy heart. (Isaiah 61:1–3)

You have turned my laments into dancing; **you have stripped off my sackcloth and clothed me with joy**, that I may sing psalms to you without ceasing. LORD my God, I shall praise you forever. (Psalm 30:11, emphasis supplied)

Clearly, we are not left alone to deal with our emotions. Some of us are naturally upbeat and can always see the silver lining. Others easily see the dark side of things and think being optimistic is unrealistic. But God calls us all to walk in His presence and experience His joy and His power. Listen to David's song of gratitude in 1 Chronicles 16:

Exult in his hallowed name; **let those who seek the LORD be joyful in heart. Look to the LORD and be strong; at all times seek his presence**. (vv. 10–11, emphasis supplied)

Sing to the LORD, all the earth, **proclaim his victory day by day**. Declare his glory among the nations, his marvellous deeds to every people. (vv. 23–24, emphasis supplied)

Majesty and splendour attend him, **might and joy are in his dwelling**. (v. 27, emphasis supplied)

Take Care of Yourself!

Particularly during difficult times, it's important that we take the time to give our minds and bodies what they need to remain healthy, or we will become susceptible to a variety of physical and emotional ailments. One of these, depression, has reached epidemic proportions.

Nevertheless, we often refuse to acknowledge depression, afraid that people will view us as too weak to deal with the normal stresses of life. Many believe it's just a part of life. Fortunately, it can be easy to manage by simply taking care of yourself.

Dr. Neal Nedley, an internist who practices in California, has researched the causes of depression and developed some straightforward techniques for treating it. He describes ten factors involved in the illness. Depression can result when any four of these factors hit you simultaneously. Only three are beyond your control: genetic, developmental, and social factors. Generally, we are able to manage the other seven: nutrition, toxins, circadian rhythm (adequate sleep), addiction, lifestyle choices, medical conditions, and frontal lobe (cognitive thinking). Effectively managing these factors can dramatically impact the occurrence of depression. He's written some excellent books on the subject, *Proof Positive* and *Depression: A Way Out*. Even if you've never suffered from depression or are one of the most optimistic people in the world, following the steps he delineates will boost your spirits. Take a look at his website at drnedley.com.

If we're claiming God's promises to bring healing, shouldn't we first eliminate self-destructive habits from our lives? Yet changing our habits is perhaps our biggest struggle. Habits are activities we automatically repeat, either in response to a given situation or as a part of our regular routine. But knowledge brings power. As we learn more, possibilities we might never have considered open before us. Living an abundant life doesn't require big changes all at once, but simply learning to make small, consistent choices that we repeat daily.

In short, each day, commit to putting into practice what you've learned, one small step at a time. Keep it doable. Don't create a mountain that looks too difficult to climb. Don't think about what may happen tomorrow. It's not relevant. As you progress on your journey, your feelings *will* change!

Sing Songs of Gratitude to Lift Your Spirit

"With psalms and hymns and spiritual songs, sing from the heart in gratitude to God" (Colossians 3:16). We are encouraged to sing in gratitude to God *before* we know the path He will designate or the answer He will provide.

This serves two purposes. First, it is an act of faith. We are confirming that we believe our heavenly Father's promise to always act on our behalf; we show that we believe He is eager to demonstrate His love to those who depend on Him for guidance. "Though the mountains may move and the hills shake, **my love will be immovable** and never fail, and my covenant promising peace will not be shaken, says the LORD in his pity for you" (Isaiah 54:10, emphasis supplied).

The second purpose for thanksgiving is for our protection. Satan is the ultimate example of the phrase, "Misery *loves* company." He knows what he's lost, and he knows—better than we do—that the driving force behind God's overwhelming power, consistency, and predictability is love! Satan, who has placed himself beyond God's reach, wants us to believe that we have too. Just as important, he knows we don't understand how much we have to gain. Consequently, he strives to discourage us and make us feel as if we're alone, as if God has abandoned us. If Satan can surround us with an atmosphere of gloom, if he can get us to accept destructive influences, we'll lose our grasp on God's promises. We'll believe the lie that God's promises aren't applicable to us or that we're not good enough for His attention. Satan doesn't care *how* he drags us down--he just wants to get us there.

Once overcome by despair, we become self focused—absorbed in protecting ourselves and charting our own courses for finding happiness. This leaves us completely vulnerable, and Satan can lead us wherever he wishes.

Singing and praising God for His promises from a grateful heart creates an atmosphere of worship that Satan absolutely hates. He flees! Singing when you feel down affects not only your own spirit but the atmosphere surrounding you as well. Even if you aren't a talented singer, actively praising God with your own voice makes worship personal. Listening to the music of praise whenever possible also contributes to a positive, worshipful atmosphere.

Scripture gives us two wonderful examples of the power of praise. The first is King Saul. After he had repeatedly disobeyed God's direction, the prophet Samuel told him that the throne would be passed to someone who would follow God's guidance. The Spirit of the Lord left Saul, providing a vacuum that Satan quickly filled.

For some people, this story frequently brings up other questions regarding God's actions. So, I'm going to take a brief detour. Unfortunately, the writer who chronicles Saul's story calls the spirit harassing him "an evil spirit from God" (1 Samuel 16:15). If this were the only Scripture evidence, we could draw no other conclusion. However, we know from many other verses that God does not tempt and that all his ways are loving. Here's a verse that describes the characteristics of God's spirit: "But the harvest of the Spirit is love, joy, peace, patience, kindness, goodness, fidelity, gentleness, and self-control. Against such things there is no law" (Galatians 5:22–23).

Jesus also points out that it makes no sense for God to battle Himself. In Matthew 12:22, we find Jesus healing a man who is blind, mute, and possessed by Satan. The Pharisees respond by saying that Jesus is able to heal him because he is Beelzebub, prince of the devils. In verses 26–28, he says,

> And if it is Satan who drives out Satan, he is divided against himself; how then can his kingdom stand? If it is by Beelzebub that I drive out devils, by whom do your own people drive them out? If this is your argument, they themselves will refute you. But if it is by the Spirit of God that I drive out the devils, then be sure the kingdom of God has already come upon you.

Returning to our story, once the spirit of God left Saul, he was regularly harassed by Satan. One of Saul's attendants, who was acquainted with David, gave Saul the following tip:

> 'I have seen a son of Jesse of Bethlehem who can play; he is a brave man and a good fighter, wise in speech and handsome, and the **LORD is with him**.'…And whenever an evil spirit from God came upon Saul, David would take his lyre and play it, **so that relief would come to Saul**; he would recover and the evil spirit would leave him alone. (1 Samuel 16:18, 23, emphasis supplied)

David, who clearly understood music's importance, is our second example of the power of praise. He subsequently made music that specifically praised God a key part of the temple worship service. His example became a model for the future kings of Judah. And David didn't have just a few people praising God; he had thousands praising Him. Look at the grand scale of praise he established:

> Four thousand to praise the Lord with musical instruments which David had produced for the service of praise. (1 Chronicles 23:5)

> All these were sons of Heman the king's seer, given to him through the promises of God for his greater glory. God had given Heman fourteen sons and three daughters, and they all served under their father for the singing in the house of the LORD. (1 Chronicles 25:5–6)

With such a powerful example, it makes sense that Paul would provide similar counsel to the new church of believers in Colosse.

> Always be thankful. Let the gospel of Christ dwell among you in all its richness; teach and instruct one another with all the wisdom it gives you. **With psalms and hymns and spiritual songs, sing from the heart in gratitude to God**. (Colossians 3:15–16, emphasis supplied)

Like the Colossians, we have forgotten this once well-known strategy of battling Satan's attempts to tear us down. It's so easy, yet few of us make a practice of it.

Praising God is an act of faith, something we do because we believe God loves us, knows our needs, hears our prayers, and keeps his promises. There are two dramatic examples of this in Scripture. The first is the story of King Jehoshaphat found in 2 Chronicles 20. When faced with the prospect of being attacked by a "great horde" (v. 15), he asked for God's guidance. God told him,

> 'Do not fear or be dismayed by this great horde, for the battle is in God's hands, not yours....It is not you who will fight this battle; stand firm and wait, and you will see the deliverance worked by the LORD for you, Judah and Jerusalem. Do not fear or be dismayed; go out tomorrow to face them, for the Lord is with you.' (vv. 15, 17)

Without waiting to see the outcome, Jehoshaphat and all the

people of Judah praised God for his goodness. Jehoshaphat specifically commands them, "'Hold firmly to your faith in the LORD your God and you will be upheld; have faith in his prophets and you will succeed'" (v. 20).They began to sing, "'Give thanks to the Lord, for his love endures forever'" (v. 21). As soon as the attacking armies heard the "loud shouts of praise" (v. 23), they savagely turned on each other until none were left alive!

The second story is about King Hezekiah's restoration of worship to God and the subsequent healing of the people (2 Chronicles 29–31). As Moses had predicted years earlier, Israel had turned their backs on God and had begun worshipping the gods of the surrounding nations. King Hezekiah called the Levites to rededicate themselves, restore the services of the sanctuary, and call the people of Israel and Judah back to worshipping God. As ordered by King David, the Levites were stationed in the house of the Lord with cymbals, lutes, and lyres and they sang and praised God joyfully. In chapter 30, we see King Hezekiah praying that every person that "makes a practice" (v. 19) of seeking God's guidance be healed. God heard the king's prayer and the people were healed! There was great rejoicing and praise with *"unrestrained fervour!"* (v. 21).

If we wait for things to be worked out the way we want before we praise God, that's hardly a testimony of our confidence in His power and loving kindness. On the other hand, if those around us hear us praising God *before* the way is opened, they will be impressed with our confidence in our heavenly Father. Please also note: praising Him doesn't mean we're praising Him because He's going to open the door as we see fit. We're praising Him because we know the door He opens will be for our benefit at this particular point in our lives. Frequently, we can't see the benefit of the course God puts us on until later. Praising God before we have this knowledge affirms His care and acknowledges our limited knowledge and power. "You keep close guard behind and before me and place your hand upon me. Knowledge so wonderful is beyond my grasp; it is so lofty I cannot reach it" (Psalm 139:5–6).

Share What God Is Teaching You

"I have not kept your goodness hidden in my heart; I have proclaimed your faithfulness and saving power, and have not concealed your unfailing love and truth from the great assembly" (Psalm 40:10). I'm sure you'll agree that these scriptures are like gems—priceless finds that bring a renewed sense of hope. God's way is straightforward and simple; yet it has been so tragically muddled and complicated. As His way lights up your life, you're told to share it with those within your sphere of influence.

You'll find that this sharing happens naturally and spontaneously; you can't keep it to yourself. You'll see people struggling with the same problems you've struggled with, so you can see the direction the Lord wants to take them. You'll want them to know about God's love and faithfulness, because you want them to experience the joy it's brought to your life. You'll want them to know that the fear and doubt they're struggling with is unnecessary.

As you share, your joy becomes even greater. No one has to teach you how to share. It's *your* experience; it just bubbles up from within you! You can't suppress it. By His Spirit working through you, God is able to provide healing to those with whom you share. You will see the words of Isaiah 61:1–3 come true:

> The spirit of the Lord GOD is upon me because the LORD has anointed me; he has sent me to announce good news to the humble, **to bind up the broken-hearted**, to proclaim liberty to captives, release to those in prison; to proclaim a year of the LORD's favour and a day of the vengeance of our God; to comfort all who mourn, to give them garlands instead of ashes, **oil of gladness instead of mourners' tears, a garment of splendour for the heavy heart**.

Sharing also reaffirms your faith. Talking about your experience helps strengthen you in the new path you're walking. It also helps you remember what God has done in your life.

Keep Repeating this Process!

You'll find you must keep repeating this process with each new challenge you meet. With every new situation, you will be challenged to move out of your comfort zone once again. You'll find yourself asking God to provide direction and assistance in completely new ways. So, even though you know the steps you must take, it will continue to feel like a new experience. With each new experience, the bar may get higher. You may even find that you'll wait longer for the answer. As you move forward, your faith will deepen. You'll also discover that you are ministering more to others. My hope is that you'll learn this process faster than I have!

Commit your way to the LORD; trust in him, and he will act. He will make your righteousness shine clear as the day and the justice of your cause like the brightness of noon. (Psalm 37:5–6)

> They who look to him are radiant with joy; they will never be put out of countenance. Here is one who cried out in his affliction; the LORD heard him and saved him from all his troubles. (Psalm 34:5–6)

Action Steps

1. Become conscious of God's voice and Satan's voice. Contrast their messages.

2. Write down the words of at least two praise songs or hymns that encourage you.

3. Identify an accountability partner with whom you can pray and who can gently remind you of the promises when you express doubt.

4. Of the stories in Scripture that you've read, which is your favorite? Why?

5. Are the concepts presented difficult to believe? Why?

6. Which of the steps reviewed in this chapter will be most difficult for you to use? Why?

Additional Scripture for Study

1. Revelation 21:8: What are the first two characteristics listed? How prevalent are these traits inside the church?

2. Read: Daniel 1, 3; Nehemiah 1–2. Do you think that Daniel and Nehemiah had reasons to doubt? How do you think they dealt with their challenging situations? What lesson can you learn?

Chapter 5

In His Presence

Hidden Gem:

When Abram was ninety-nine years old, the LORD appeared to him and said, 'I am God Almighty. Live always in my presence and be blameless, so that I may make my covenant with you and give you many descendants.' (Genesis 17:1–2)

As a sophomore in college, I was frustrated by inorganic chemistry. It didn't matter how hard I studied, I couldn't seem to score much better than a C-plus. Midway through the first quarter, Professor Webster distributed everyone's exam except mine. He asked that I meet him after class. He asked me a question from the exam and I answered correctly. He then showed me the answer that I'd written. To my surprise, my answer wasn't even close. Dr. Webster had observed my class participation; he had seen how I was helping other students understand the material; he had also noticed that they were getting better grades than me! He easily saw that I had a bad case of nerves and poor self-esteem.

What was obvious to Dr. Webster, I couldn't see at all. His willingness to pull me aside and give me the counsel I needed at that critical point in my life was invaluable. Our relationship continued to grow until he was like my father away from home. His insight into my strengths and weaknesses was the first step toward improving my self-confidence. The condition necessary for this blessing was my being in his presence.

We're called to remain in God's presence, rejoice over His marvelous acts, and recognize that every word He speaks is given to bless us. Having a correct concept of God frees us to embrace right choices without feeling that we are somehow sacrificing our happiness. It also means that the more we know of God's counsel, the more we'll be blessed and enjoy better quality of life. This is the meaning of thirsting after righteousness. It means we can't get enough of God's goodness. But, to avoid being accountable to God, sometimes we don't want to know too much.

Will we make the mental shift and embrace this simple concept that will transform our lives? Trusting God becomes a whole lot easier! Until we take this step, we will not progress. Christ's words sum up what God's intention has always been: "I have come that they may have life, and may have it in all its fullness" (John 10:10). None of this is new; we've just now finally gotten it!

A joyful, trusting heart that desires obedience because it understands God's intentions is radically different from the heart that obeys just to get to heaven. This isn't trust! The person whose life is built around forced actions and constant constraints will never be happy because he feels he's been deprived of something. Besides, forced behavior doesn't last. It will just be a matter of time before the person falls back into their old path. What a miserable existence! Who wants to follow that path? It results in all kinds of dysfunctional behavior.

For example, I've worked in healthcare most of my career and have heard many physicians express their frustration over seeing so many patients who will not make positive lifestyle choices that would dramatically improve their health. I've seen the underwriting data that demonstrates that 60 to 80 percent of all costs incurred could be avoided if people would change their lifestyle. How's that for a simple solution to America's healthcare crisis? This is the white elephant in the room that no one dares to talk about.

However, when you talk with someone who is suffering from the results of their choices, what do you commonly hear? "Well, I have to die from something, so I might as well die enjoying my vices!" Or, "Why is God allowing this to happen to me?"

They ask the doctor for a magic cure so they can continue the same lifestyle without any of the negative effects. This, of course, is impossible! They view the recommended change as a negative—as if they are giving up something. They would rather suffer the effects of a debilitating and life threatening disease than feel good and live longer. They're unable to view the change as something that will enrich their lives.

We all know the verse from Proverbs: "A cheerful heart is good medicine" (Proverbs 17:22 NLT). The person who thrives is the person who sees the change they're making as positive and happily embraces it with no regrets.

An equally unfortunate outcome is happening in churches. There's a growing level of dysfunctional behavior within the church that goes uncorrected. As a result, people's lives are hurt, and a whole generation doesn't understand the simplicity, power, and joy of the gospel message. Why? People look for reasons to justify not taking God at His word. This attitude encourages them to ignore the bad choices they're making today and focus instead on the end prize, which is heaven. The pastor in a church like this is really saying, "God accepts you where you are today, the way you are now. Some time in the future, He'll forcibly change you into the person you never desired to be today." We see the results of this kind of thinking in the increasing numbers of church members participating in extramarital affairs, divorce, and dishonesty.

Instead of uplifting God as a loving God who desires to transform us now, this attitude portrays Him as a God who loves us but overlooks our dysfunctional behavior. He isn't interested in blessing our day-to-day existence; He just promises heaven...eventually.

This means a beautifully simple message, the eternal gospel, has been distorted into an illogical, complicated mess. It robs God of demonstrating His relevance and power, and it robs us of seeing His love and grace in action. This inflicts excruciating pain on God, who must now watch His child walk down a path guaranteed to bring her pain and sorrow!

Look at God's emotional response to Israel's failure to understand: "I am wounded by my people's wound; I go about in mourning, overcome with horror....Would that my head were a spring of water, my eyes a fountain of tears, that I might weep day and night for the slain of my people" (Jeremiah 8:21; 9:1).

Nevertheless, God never gives up on us. God paints for Ezekiel a gruesome picture of Israel's condition in order to demonstrate the transformation He desires to make in their lives.

> The LORD's hand was upon me, and he carried me out by his spirit and set me down in a plain that was full of bones. He made me pass among them in every direction. Countless in number and very dry, they covered the plain. He said to me, 'O man, can these bones live?' I answered, 'Only you, Lord GOD, know that.' He said, 'Prophesy over these bones; say: Dry bones, hear the word of the LORD. The Lord GOD says to these bones: I am going to put breath into you, and you will live. I shall fasten sinews on you, clothe you with flesh, cover you with skin, and give you breath, and you will live. Then you will know that I am the LORD.'" (Ezekiel 37:1–6)

God's message is simple: it's never too late for Him to demonstrate His transforming power.

As I've learned to trust and embrace positive choices, I've begun to see positive growth in my life. These blessings bring joy to my heart. No theological argument can dispute what I *know* and have seen God do for me and in the lives of those around me. When someone trusts God, he will make positive choices. "These are the words of the Lord GOD, the Holy One of Israel: In calm detachment lies your safety, your strength in quiet trust....Yet the Lord is waiting to show you his favour, and he yearns to have pity on you; for the LORD is a God of justice. Happy are all who wait for him!" (Isaiah 30:15, 18).

Whenever we see people who have trusted God and waited for Him to act, we see their spirit of gratitude and awe erupt into songs of praise. It doesn't matter if He's delivered them, guided them, or provided for their needs; the reaction is the same. Examples include:

➢ Moses and the Israelites singing to the Lord when God delivered them from the Egyptians at the Red Sea (Exodus 15:1–21)

➢ Deborah, Barak, and the Israelites singing after God's victory over the Canaanites (Judges 5)

- ➤ Hannah's prayer of thanksgiving when the prophet Samuel was born (1 Samuel 2:1–10)
- ➤ King David's song of thanksgiving when God delivered him from King Saul (2 Samuel 22:2–51)
- ➤ King David and the Israelites rejoicing when the Ark of the Covenant returns to Jerusalem (1 Chronicles 16:7–36)
- ➤ Israel's thanksgiving over the generous donation of materials to build God's temple (1 Chronicles 29:10–14)
- ➤ The twenty-four elders surrounding God's throne, who praise Him unceasingly day and night. Laying their crowns before Him, they cry, "'You are worthy, O Lord our God, to receive glory and honour and power, because you created all things; by your will they were created and have their being!'" (Revelation 4:11)

If only there were more people walking the path of joyful obedience! Such people give an accurate picture of our heavenly Father that creates a desire in others to duplicate this experience. The people walking this path are dramatically different in their attitudes. They don't see joyful obedience as a sacrifice! They have nothing to complain about! They know that their God is in control and is guiding them on a journey that will leave them awestruck.

I find it both intriguing and unsettling that my lack of faith prevents God from doing what He really wants to do in my life. It's a challenge to wrap my head around the idea that each of us has a personal call to come into His presence, hear His voice, and know His guiding hand in our individual lives. God's promise to guide us on a unique journey *is* His call to salvation. Our willingness to trustingly obey His counsel and direction *is* our salvation. God can't force me; it's my life.

This is an important point that has broad implications. It means we each choose how much of God's glory we'll experience. It also means we will be impacted by both our choices and other people's choices when we fail to seek and follow God's guidance. The concept of salvation takes on a much broader meaning.

We now have the opportunity to accept a call similar to Abraham's, to "go to a country that I will show you" (Genesis 12:1). By dwelling with God, Abraham received a specific call to action. His decision to follow God's counsel was evidence of His faith in God. There was no doctrinal debate.

> Faith gives substance to our hopes and convinces us of realities we do not see....By faith Abraham obeyed the call to leave his home for a land which he was to receive as a possession; he went away without knowing where he was to go. By faith he settled as an alien in the land which had been promised him, living in tents with Isaac and Jacob, who were heirs with him to the same promise. (Hebrews 11:1, 8–9)

We've not learned to dwell with God; consequently, many of us don't know the special call He has for our lives. Since God doesn't impose, learning to hear His voice requires determination and focus. It doesn't just happen. We must ask. This leaves us in the rather uncomfortable position of having to acknowledge that we're the problem; we're our own worst enemies. Following a simple checklist of "dos and don'ts" is much easier. Our insistence on doing things the easy way keeps us from living the life we've always wanted to live. God's commandments are unifying principles that apply to us all; however, they are just the starting point.

It's so much easier to go about our business, giving lip service to "Jesus is Lord of my life" while searching for a path that allows us to do what we want while still being assured of going to heaven. This way, we don't have to learn to listen to His voice. It's so much easier to focus on creating our own comfortable list of things to do. We face a whole new challenge when we understand that a saving faith believes that God's counsel is always for our benefit and that He wants to begin transforming us into His image today as we follow His voice. The very thought is humbling, causing us to feel our need of His grace to make this process a reality.

All this is achieved by dwelling in *His* presence where we can't compare ourselves to anyone else or depend upon our pastor, priest, bishop, or reverend. When we talk with God, it's between Him and us—no one else.

To dwell in His presence means to take the time to slow down, hear His small, still voice, and then obey it. When there's so much pressure to maximize our productivity, taking time to slow down is an act of faith in itself. Christ said, "My own sheep listen to my voice; I know them and they follow me" (John 10:27). His call frequently stretches us, requiring that we stay connected to Him. His calling creates a healthy humility.

Moses understood this. He asked God to find someone else to bring the children of Israel to the Promised Land. Yet, forty years earlier, he was confident that he had the skill to accomplish it. Now, he was no longer so sure of himself. It wasn't even his dream anymore. When God insisted he was the man for the job, Moses felt a tremendous need to stay connected:

> 'If I have won your favour, then teach me to know your ways, so that I can know you and continue in favour with you, for this nation is your own people.' The LORD answered, 'I shall go myself and set your mind at rest.' Moses said to him, 'Indeed if you do not go yourself, do not send us up from here; for how can it ever be known that I and your people have found favour with you, except by your going with us? So we shall be distinct, I and your people, from all the peoples on earth.' (Exodus 33:13–16)

What we do is a reflection of what we believe. Moses believed, and his actions reflected his faith. This is what James means when he says in James 2:26, "As the body is dead when there is no breath left in it, so faith divorced from action is dead." Since the days of Martin Luther, the Christian church has struggled over the meaning of this verse. Based upon what Martin Luther knew and the culture of his day, his struggle was understandable. For us, it is not. The information available to us is mind-boggling.

Many authors have applied this concept in self-help books, and they have done it without harnessing the power of God's grace! What's this magic concept? In order to achieve tangible results, you must first identify the steps needed to reach your goal, and then execute your plan. Otherwise, you have only good intentions. Intentions not followed up by action are dreams that will never come true. In other words, faith without action means you really don't have any faith.

Now just imagine: we have the opportunity to partner with our

Creator and achieve things that we've yet to even imagine! This is what God's grace is all about. Transformation is restoration, and restoration is healing. Sin has kept us blind and prevented us from fulfilling God's vision, but God's grace heals. "For the grace of God has dawned upon the world with healing for all mankind" (Titus 2:11).

These verses put us on edge; they encourage us to view God differently, to listen to His voice as it reminds us of the direction He wishes to take us. We're forced to confront what's going on in our life today—not what we wish someone else would do but what we *know* we are called to do. And we *do* know! We have all heard His small, still voice.

His voice comforts, heals, challenges, and directs us. This ongoing process fulfills the promises recorded by Jeremiah and John. Note the similarities between these passages:

> "This is the new covenant I will make with the people of Israel on that day," says the LORD. "I will put my laws in their minds, and I will write them on their hearts. I will be their God, and they will be my people. And they will not need to teach their neighbors, nor will they need to teach their family, saying, 'You should know the LORD.' For everyone, from the least to the greatest, will already know me," says the LORD. "And I will forgive their wickedness and will never remember their sins." (Jeremiah 31:33–34 NLT)

> What is more, you have been anointed by the Holy One, and so you all have knowledge....But as for you, the anointing which you received from Him remains with you; you need no other teacher, but you learn all you need to know from his anointing, which is true and no lie. **Dwell in him as he taught you to do**." (1 John 2:20, 27, emphasis supplied)

The results of our learning to dwell in Him are also comparable. Look at the similarities in the following verses:

> Whoever claims to be dwelling in him must live as Christ himself lived. (1 John 2:6)

As the Father has loved me, so I have loved you. Dwell in my love. If you heed my commands, you will dwell in my love, as I have heeded my Father's commands and dwell in his love. (John 15:9–10)

In a word, as God's dear children, you must be like him. (Ephesians 5:1)

Live always in my presence and be blameless.(Genesis 17:1)

After the birth of Methuselah, Enoch walked with God for three hundred years, and had other sons and daughters. He lived three hundred and sixty-five years. Enoch walked with God, and then was seen no more, because God had taken him away. (Genesis 5:22)

God has consistently invited us to dwell with Him. His invitation is not new. We find Enoch walking with God. Enoch and God became so close that God took him to heaven, and Enoch could no longer be found. We see the invitation given to Abraham to dwell with God and be blameless. In Exodus 19, God invites all of Israel to Mt. Sinai to meet with Him. After all the elders ate with God in Exodus 24, He asks Moses to build a sanctuary that He might dwell among the Israelites. In Revelation 21, when those who have total confidence in God and have learned to trust Him to reach heaven, there's a sense that God's ultimate dream has finally come true. "I heard a loud voice proclaiming from the throne: 'Now God has his dwelling with mankind! **He will dwell among them and they shall be his people**, and God himself will be with them'" (Revelation 21:3, emphasis supplied).

The exclamation point clearly conveys the feeling that He has always longed to dwell with us; however, He has been unable to experience this joy because of our choices. With similar intensity, when Israel left Egypt, He called them to be His special possession. God invites us, "If only you will now listen to me and keep my covenant, then out of all peoples you will become my special possession; for the whole earth is mine. You will be to me a kingdom of priests, my holy nation" (Exodus 19:5–6).

We demonstrate our lack of faith by attempting to explain away the simple clarity of these verses. There's nothing to misunderstand. There's no symbolism.

Some people say that God set Israel up for a fall, that it was impossible for them to observe His covenant and statutes, just as it's impossible for us to observe them today. This explanation is ridiculous for two reasons.

First, Moses states in no uncertain terms, "This commandment that I lay on you today is not too difficult for you or beyond your reach.... It is a thing very near to you, on your lips and **in your heart** ready to be kept" (Deuteronomy 30:11, 14, emphasis supplied). Here's an example of God's grace actively at work. When they allowed God to dwell with them, he placed the ability to observe His statutes in their hearts. They had to choose to come, to remain, and to believe that His commandments and statutes were given for their benefit—not His. Upon taking these steps of coming and staying in His presence, they would receive an everlasting gift: a transformed heart.

Second, as we've mentioned before, the statutes were specifically given to create a functional and harmonious society that the surrounding nations would admire and be drawn to copy. They would have said, "'What a wise and understanding people this great nation is!' What great nation has a god close at hand as the LORD our God is close to us whenever we call to him?" (Deuteronomy 4:6–7). Now, what possible reason would God have for creating a vision of a functional, harmonious society if there was no hope of achieving it? Failure was their choice, not God's!

The book of Deuteronomy records Moses' last words of counsel to Israel before he died. He summarizes the previous forty years, lists the lessons they learned, and gives counsel for the future.

God is dealing with a group of people who have been slaves for a long time. He outlines the reasons he gave them the law and tells them what kind of impact they will have on the surrounding nations if they follow those laws. God also promises that if they follow His laws and keep the covenant, He will bless them. He repeats this same promise twenty times in Deuteronomy!

As you read this book, you'll see that there's simply no room to place any blame on God. I've concluded that we are no different from Israel. He's promised to provide all of our needs. We must simply believe that He means what He says. There's no downside risk, nothing to sacrifice, and nothing to give up! Failing to take this step means that we don't *really* believe that our God is all-powerful, that He really wants to transform us, and that He can make us more than we can possibly imagine.

To be blunt, when we decide not to take this step, we are really saying that we just want to do things our way. We want to have what we want without any negative consequences.

As a body, Christianity has lost its passion for entering into His presence and embracing His counsel. Instead, we have decided to give people excuses for inappropriate behavior. This is why we do not experience God's power in our lives. It is why the church has lost its relevance. "The LORD replied, 'Is there a limit to the power of the LORD? You will now see whether or not my words come true'" (Numbers 11:23). "I am the LORD, the God of all mankind; is anything impossible for me?" (Jeremiah 32:27).

No, there is no limit to God's power!

God's promise to Israel through Moses was conditional upon obedience. Christ's promise to us is also conditional. "'Anyone who has received my commands and obeys them—he it is who loves me; and he who loves me will be loved by my Father; and I will love him and disclose myself to him'" (John 14:21).

When we come into His presence, we are changed. Then our witness changes those around us by our prayers and our actions.

We must *choose* to stay in His presence, and this is as challenging as our first step of faith. Why is it such a challenge? As God begins to touch our lives, we are grateful for the positive change He brings. Some are satisfied with the change but don't understand that there's much more He wants to accomplish. Their vision is too limited. Others confuse God's actions with their abilities. Instead of a spirit of gratitude, a spirit of pride begins to grow within them. This can quickly replace the spirit of faith that started them on their journey.

Moses warned Israel of this when he told them,

> Do not become proud and forget the LORD your God who brought you out of Egypt, out of that land of slavery.... Nor must you say to yourselves, 'My own strength and energy have gained me this wealth.' Remember the LORD

your God; it is he who gives you strength to become prosperous, so fulfilling the covenant guaranteed by oath with your forefathers, as he does to this day....He is your proud boast. (Deuteronomy 8:14, 17–18; 10:21)

The forty years Moses spent as a shepherd humbled him. He's called "the most humble man on earth" (Numbers 12:3). We too need a healthy dose of humility to remember our need to stay in His presence. Scripture compares our continuing need to dwell in His presence to our continuing need for water.

Let me remind you, my friends, that our ancestors were all under the cloud, and all of them passed through the Red Sea; so they all received baptism into the fellowship of Moses in cloud and sea. They all ate the same supernatural food, and all drank the same supernatural drink; for they drank from the supernatural rock that accompanied their travels—and that rock was Christ. (1 Corinthians 10:1–4)

The LORD is my shepherd; I lack for nothing. He makes me lie down in green pastures, **he leads me to water where I may rest**; he revives my spirit; for his name's sake he guides me in the right paths. (Psalm 23:1–3, emphasis supplied)

They are filled with the rich plenty of your house, and you give them to drink from the stream of your delights; for **with you is the fountain of life**, and by your light we are enlightened. (Psalm 36:8–9, emphasis supplied)

Blessed is anyone who trusts in the LORD, and rests his confidence on him. He will be **like a tree planted by the waterside**, that sends out its roots along a stream. When the heat comes it has nothing to fear; its foliage stays green. Without care in a year of drought, it does not fail to bear fruit....LORD, on whom Israel's hope is fixed, all who reject you will be put to shame; those who forsake you will be inscribed in the dust, for they have rejected the **source of living water, the LORD**. (Jeremiah 17:7–8, 13, emphasis supplied)

Jesus answered, 'Everyone who drinks this water will be thirsty again; but whoever drinks the water I shall give will never again be thirsty. The water that I shall give will be **a spring of water** within him, welling up and bringing eternal life.' (John 4:13–14, emphasis supplied)

My people have committed two sins: they have rejected me, **a source of living water**, and they have hewn out for themselves cisterns, cracked cisterns which hold no water. (Jeremiah 2:13, emphasis supplied)

'Come!' say the Spirit and the bride. 'Come!' let each hearer reply. Let the thirsty come; let whoever wishes **accept the water of life as a gift**. (Revelation 22:17, emphasis supplied)

Moses summed these scriptures up in a single verse that Jesus quoted when he met Satan in the wilderness: "That people cannot live on bread alone, but that they live on every word that comes from the mouth of the LORD" (Deuteronomy 8:3). As we make a habit of drinking regularly, we will crave God's presence like water, knowing our need for being in His presence. This is why Moses insisted that God go with him, why Daniel prayed three times each day, and why Jesus withdrew from the crowds to spend time with our Father.

While we're in His presence, He speaks to us. His message is uniquely ours. His commands are not limited to the Ten Commandments given at Mt. Sinai, but include His unique guidance for our lives. After all, each of us has a unique set of talents. So, why should this sound far-fetched?

Consider what would have happened if Abraham had not left his country. Think of the impact his willingness to act had on his family and on the surrounding community. What would have happened if he had not chosen to sacrifice Isaac? What would have happened if Aaron had not gone to meet Moses? Or if Peter had decided he wanted to remain a fisherman? What would have happened if Elijah had chosen not to take the meat given him by the ravens? The guidance God gave each of these men was unique—just for him.

These people had reason to object to God's guidance and continue doing what they believed to be rational. Certainly Abraham's family questioned the wisdom of his departure, especially when he had no idea where he was going. Don't you think Abraham had some doubts when God told him to sacrifice Isaac? Don't you think he wondered if it was a mistake? After all, would a loving God ask him to murder his own son? Don't you think Aaron had doubts about Moses' ability to return to Egypt and leave again alive? Or that Elijah had questions when God asked him to eat the meat provided him by a raven—a scavenger? I'm sure each of these men questioned whether it was God's voice they were hearing.

God had a unique command for each of these individuals—commands that seemed far-fetched. Their decision to act and to trust God affected millions of people who witnessed God's power through successive generations. Since God is no respecter of persons, and He desires that we be restored in His image, what makes us think He doesn't want to use each of us in a mighty way right now? If you consider this, Christ's faith-stretching challenge makes sense:

> In very truth I tell you, whoever has faith in me will do what I am doing; **indeed he will do greater things still because I am going to the Father**. Anything you ask in my name I will do, so that the Father may be glorified in the Son. **If you ask anything in my name I will do it**. (John 14:12–14, emphasis supplied)

Where did this story start? It started as a simple answer of faith to the question the Lord asked Abraham and Sarah in Genesis 18:14: "Is anything impossible for the LORD?"

God told Moses, "See that you listen, and do all that I command you, and then it will go well with you and your children after you forever" (Deuteronomy 12:28). *We must accept that all God's ways are for our benefit!* Without being grounded in this simple concept, we are paralyzed by an experience that lacks the power, the transformation, and the joy that God intends.

A paralyzed experience prevents us from experiencing the power of God in our lives. We rationalize why we don't see the promises come true and minimize the role God wants to play in our lives. We no longer take His promises literally, we see His counsel as overdone, out of step, harsh, and unrealistic, and we postpone the expectation of deliverance and growth to some undefined future date. We *must* rationalize to reconcile our belief in an all-powerful God with our reality, which contains no visible sign of His involvement. In short, it's our way of making ourselves feel better, of quieting the inner voice that screams that we're missing out.

When this happens with large numbers of people, Christianity becomes a cultural experience. With the apparent absence of God, it becomes just another belief system to be defended. This fosters the growth of two extremes: legalism and liberalism.

Legalism uses God's law as a checklist to confirm that His requirements have all been met. It makes God look harsh, rigid, unfeeling, and unmerciful, but enables the person to feel good about himself. On the other extreme, liberalism misrepresents God's grace, removing the power of choice and the expectation that God transforms lives. Legalism breeds an atmosphere of intolerance, guilt, and impatience, while liberalism breeds an atmosphere of disorganization and low expectations. To the liberal, loving someone means turning your head and ignoring or tolerating unacceptable behavior. Both bring disastrous results, all in the name of a loving heavenly Father!

Furthermore, both extremes encourage atheism. Those looking in from the outside see no reason to join such a guilt-ridden, critical, dysfunctional group of people. They certainly see no convincing evidence that God exists in the lives of these people. Instead, they see people with the same problems they have, people who appear no happier and who have no better solutions. They have merely embraced a philosophy that causes them to deny the reality of life's stresses instead of effectively dealing with their problems. Many see Christians as people who make excuses for bad behavior. This is why Karl Marx called Christianity the "opiate of the masses."

For kids who grow up in this environment, the fear of future consequences for being disobedient (hell or being eternally lost) does not deter them from making poor choices. They believe they can finally find joy and happiness—something they see missing in their parent's lives—outside of God. They don't want to be like their parents. They are determined not to repeat their parents' mistakes; yet, apart from God, they are destined for the same result.

Does this mean that the individual actively learning to dwell with

God is not looking forward to heaven? Absolutely not! So what's the difference between the child of faith and the rationalizer? The more the child of faith enjoys dwelling with God, the more clearly he sees the terrible results of sin and its accompanying pain. Peter captures their feelings in 2 Peter 2:7–8:

> But he rescued Lot, a good man distressed by the dissolute habits of the lawless society in which he lived; day after day every sight and sound of their evil ways tortured that good man's heart.

The more time they spend with God, the more they see the changes that need to be made in their own lives. As He answers their prayers and they experience the positive changes that result, a spirit of compassion and tolerance towards others grows within them. As they connect with people who have never experienced the joy of trusting God, they feel a sense of empathy and sadness that results in them sharing God's goodness naturally. It's spontaneous—a reflection of their gratitude for what God has done in their lives. It's not seen as a duty, nor is it condescending or condemning. The listener feels that the concern expressed is heartfelt.

Children of faith look forward to the promise of heaven. It's a place to build friendships with those who love trusting God. Increasingly, they dream of physically being in God's presence. It's a dream they can hardly wait to see realized. They will no longer hear Satan's voice tempting, taunting, and condemning them. Fear of death has no part in the decisions they make to trust God. They have learned by experience that there is no joy outside of His presence.

Those who have come to experience the joy of dwelling with Him see heaven in its appropriate perspective. They look forward with hopeful anticipation to finally being in the presence of the One who has consistently loved, guided, delivered, and transformed them beyond their expectations.

And I heard what sounded like a vast throng, like the sound of a mighty torrent or of great peals of thunder, and they cried: 'Hallelujah! The Lord our God, sovereign over all, has entered on his reign! Let us rejoice and shout for joy and pay homage to him, for the wedding day of the Lamb has come! His bride has made herself ready, and she has been given fine linen, shining and clean, to wear.' (The fine linen signifies the righteous deeds of God's people.) (Revelation 19:6–8)

Action Steps

1. Identify ways you can slow down. Make a list. Be prepared—making these changes will be more difficult than you think. Make small changes at a time.

2. Write down your prayer requests. You may find that your mind drifts or you get sleepy. Praying aloud will really help. Sing before you pray; this also helps.

3. Begin reading the book of Deuteronomy (see the Deuteronomy Study Guide at the end of this book).

4. As you begin to notice positive changes in your life, share them with your children. Show them how to begin their own journey. Share the promises.

Additional Scripture for Study

1. Isaiah 40:8–9; 41:13–14; 44:21–23

2. Ezekiel 33:30–32

3. Romans 8:10–16, 29–32 and 15:13

4. Colossians 1:9–12

5. 2 Peter 1:3–10

The Promise Moses Repeated Over and Over in Deuteronomy

1. You must keep his statutes and his commands which I give you today; so all will be well with you and with your children after you, and you will enjoy long life in the land which the Lord your God is giving you for all time. (Deuteronomy 4:40)

2. Would that they may always be of a mind to fear me and observe my commandments, so that all will be well with them and their children forever! (Deuteronomy 5:29)

3. You must be careful to do as the Lord your God has commanded you; do not deviate from it to right or to left. You must conform to all the Lord your God commands you, if you would live and prosper and remain long in the land you are to occupy. (Deuteronomy 5:32–33)

4. If you listen, Israel, and are careful to observe them, you will prosper and increase greatly as the Lord the God of your forefathers promised you. (Deuteronomy 6:3)

5. You must do what is right and good in the eyes of the Lord, so that all may go well with you, and you may enter and occupy the good land which the Lord promised on oath to your forefathers. (Deuteronomy 6:18)

6. The Lord commanded us to observe all these statutes and to fear the Lord our God; it will be for our own good at all times, and he will continue to preserve our lives. (Deuteronomy 6:24)

7. Because you listen to these laws and are careful to observe them, the Lord your God will observe the sworn covenant he made with your forefathers and will keep faith with you. He will love you, bless you, and increase your numbers. He will bless the fruit of your body and the fruit of your soil, your grain and new wine and oil, the young of your herds and lambing flocks, in the land which he swore to your forefathers he would give you. (Deuteronomy 7:12–13)

8. You must carefully observe every command I give you this day so that you may live and increase in numbers and enter and occupy the land which the LORD promised on oath to your forefathers. (Deuteronomy 8:1)

9. What then, Israel, does the LORD your God ask of you? Only this: to fear the LORD your God, to conform to all his ways, to love him, and to serve him with all your heart and soul. This you will do by observing the commandments of the LORD and his statutes which I give you this day for your good. (Deuteronomy 10:12–13)

10. Observe all the commands I give you this day, so that you may have the strength to enter and occupy the land into which you are about to cross, and so that you may enjoy long life in the land which the LORD swore to your forefathers to give them and their descendants, a land flowing with milk and honey. (Deuteronomy 11:8–9)

11. If you pay heed to the commandments which I give you this day, to love the LORD your God and serve him with all your heart and soul, then I shall send rain for your land in season, both autumn and spring rains, and you will gather your corn and new wine and oil, and I shall provide pasture in the fields for your cattle: you will have all you want to eat. (Deuteronomy 11:13–15)

12. Take these commandments of mine to heart and keep them in mind. Bind them as a sign on your hands and wear them as a pendant on your foreheads....Then you will live long, you and your children, in the land which the LORD swore to your forefathers to give them, for as long as the heavens are above the earth. (Deuteronomy 11:18,21)

13. See that you listen, and do all that I command you, and then it will go well with you and your children after you forever; for you will be doing what is good and right in the eyes of the LORD your God. (Deuteronomy 12:28)

14. There will never be any poor among you if only you obey the LORD your God by carefully keeping these commandments which I lay upon you this day; for the LORD your God will bless you with great prosperity in the land which he is giving you to occupy as your holding.When the LORD your God blesses you, as he promised, you will lend to people of many nations, but you yourselves will

borrow from none; you will rule many nations, but none will rule you. (Deuteronomy 15:4–6)

15. The LORD has recognized you this day as his special possession, as he promised you, and you are to keep all his commandments; high above all the nations which he has made he will raise you, to bring him praise and fame and glory, and to be a people holy to the LORD your God, according to his promise. (Deuteronomy 26:18–19)

16. The LORD will establish you as his own holy people, as he swore to you, provided you keep the commandments of the LORD your God and conform to his ways. All people on earth seeing that the LORD has named you as his very own will go in fear of you. The LORD will make you prosper greatly in the fruit of your body and of your cattle, and in the fruit of the soil in the land which he swore to your forefathers to give you. May the LORD open the heavens for you, his rich storehouse, to give your land rain at the proper time and bless everything to which you turn your hand. You may lend to many nations, but borrow from none. (Deuteronomy 28:9–12)

17. Observe the provisions of this covenant and keep them so that you may be successful in all you do. (Deuteronomy 29:9)

18. If you obey the commandments of the LORD your God which I give you this day, by loving the LORD your God, conforming to his ways, and keeping his commandments, statutes, and laws, then you will live and increase, and the LORD your God will bless you in the land which you are about to enter to occupy. (Deuteronomy 30:16)

19. Love the LORD your God, obey him, and hold fast to him: that is life for you and length of days on the soil which the Lord swore to give to your forefathers, Abraham, Isaac, and Jacob. (Deuteronomy 30:20)

20. When Moses had finished reciting all these words to Israel he said: Take to heart all the warnings which I give you this day: command your children to be careful to observe all the words of this law.For you they are no empty words; they are your very life, and by them you will enjoy long life in the land which you are to occupy after crossing the Jordan. (Deuteronomy 32:45–47)

Chapter 6

It's Not All Smooth Sailing

The day finally arrived for submitting CashMap, the finance application I created for the iPad, to Apple for approval. The software development team had found the project to be more complex than we'd originally thought. But the additional three and a half months in development had been well worth the wait; we had a better finished product.

Now it was time to see how long it would take for Apple to review and approve the product. After waiting two weeks, we received notice that CashMap was in review. We'd been warned that it could take a full week for them to complete the review, and that we should expect one or two rejections before receiving final approval.

To the surprise of the whole development team, the review took a total of 90 minutes. CashMap was approved and available for sale in the iTunes App Store. As I opened the finance section, I found CashMap featured as a "New and Notable" application at the top of the page.

We were excited. The first couple of days, there were approximately

900 free downloads.We were ranked eighteenth; what an awesome start! I was being congratulated for a job well done.

CashMap's educational section was free. The cost to access the complete program was $19.99. One day, two days, three days, and finally a week went by, and I was still waiting for cash sales to begin. Our conversion rate—the proportion of people who download the free app and then buy the product—was just two percent. This was nowhere near what I'd expected.

We spent the next month making adjustments, hoping that the latest round of changes would do the trick. We watched and waited while our conversation rate inched up to 2.75 percent. Friends and finance professionals told me that we'd built a one-of-a-kind product; we had no competitors; they thought I was selling it for too little. Their positive words were not much comfort.

After investing over $400,000 from my retirement fund and from friends who had volunteered to help, I began to wonder if I'd made a terrible mistake. It had been almost two years since I was laid off. With two kids attending a private university, fear began to well up within me. As I looked at my kids, I knew that we'd been blessed. Yet, I still began to wonder if I had done the right thing. A string of questions continually raced through my head: Should we have stayed on Kauai? What should we do now? Had I acted responsibly? Should we pull our kids out of school? Should I look for work in Seattle?

> Test me, LORD, and try me, putting my heart and mind to the proof; for your constant love is before my eyes, and I live by your faithfulness. (Psalm 26:2–3)

> **He guides** the humble in right conduct, **and teaches** them his way. **All the paths of the Lord are loving and sure** to those who keep his covenant and his solemn charge.... Whoever fears the LORD will be shown the path he should choose. (Psalm 25:9–10, 12, emphasis supplied)

Moses was forty years old when he fled for his life after killing an Egyptian. He spent the next forty years taking care of sheep.Then God interrupted his tranquil life and told him to return to Egypt and lead the Israelites to the Promised Land.

To bolster Moses' confidence, God promised that he would be with him and showed Moses how to use his staff to demonstrate His power. God warned him that Pharaoh would be stubborn. Moses had no idea just how difficult it would be. He thought that once Pharaoh saw God's power, he would get the point and let Israel go. Consequently, when he faced his first set of challenges, Moses was unprepared. He was ready to head back home. He asked God two questions: "'Lord, why have you brought trouble on this people? And why did you ever send me?'" (Exodus 5:22).

Over the next forty years, Moses experienced one problem after the next. However, here's how he describes the situation: "The LORD your God has blessed you in everything you have undertaken. He has watched over your journey through this great wilderness; these forty year the Lord your God has been with you, and you have gone short of nothing" (Deuteronomy 2:7).

After reading all these wonderful promises, you may be tempted to ask, "When we exercise our faith and claim God's promises, will we be shielded from the terrible things that happen around us?" The simple answer is that sometimes we will, and sometimes we won't.

How do we know which scenario to expect? We won't! Furthermore, that shouldn't be our key focus. Instead, our attention should be on learning, with ever-increasing certainty, that God's purposes are always for our benefit. Like any relationship, this assurance only comes by experience. When we focus on allowing Him to direct our steps, we will be effective witnesses for Him in all circumstances, whether we're protected from sin's awful effects or whether we take a direct hit. The following three verses make this point powerfully:

> I do not pray you to take them out of the world, but to keep them from the evil one. (John 17:15)

> My friends, you must never tire of doing right.(2 Thessalonians 3:13)

> Always be joyful, pray continually, give thanks whatever happens; for this is what God wills for you in Christ Jesus. (1 Thessalonians 5:16–18)

Rejoicing because of what we know to be true versus how we feel is, admittedly, a real challenge. It may even sound a bit absurd. Yet, if we believe that God is with us and is cooperating for our good, we are *choosing* to act from what we know. This is faith. So often, I forget that I don't know the entire picture. My automatic response is to act as if I have all the facts. It's when I make this assumption that I question God's presence and His intentions. I forget that, as Paul Harvey used to say, "the rest of the story" will become clearer later. So, once again, we're back to the same challenge, that of ensuring that our actions reflect what we believe. This is what faith is really all about.

If you believe that God's primary focus is on who's going to make it to heaven, you won't ask yourself the question, "What changes should I make to realize the blessings God wishes to give me now?" This misdirected focus denies us the wonderfully positive process of identifying the sin in our lives and experiencing God's grace as the sin is removed.

Since we hate someone pointing out problems in our lives, we won't point out their problems. Consequently, we walk around ignoring that big white elephant in the room. Of course, if I were to point out a problem, I would dread being asked, "Are you telling me I'm not going to be saved?" I'd rather not answer that question—and appropriately so. After all, none of us have been given the role of predicting who will make it to heaven.

But the real problem is that they're asking the wrong question. God, just like any responsible parent or good friend, cares about the inevitable results of bad behavior. While it's inappropriate for me judge whether someone is going to heaven, I certainly can share with them the blessings they are missing, the inevitable long-term consequences of their choice, and the impact it may have on their relationship with their Creator.

Sometimes someone asks, "What's wrong with doing _____?" This can be an honest question, or it can be an attempt to rationalize an indefensible action. A positive response is, "God's promised a wonderful blessing when we _____." There's nothing defensive or abrasive in this response. It's encouraging people to make good choices and reinforces God's desire to bless His children. It opens an opportunity to have a positive conversation that will help the person discover promises they never knew existed. The most powerful witness is a life free of the pain resulting from disobedience. The Psalms describe the characteristics of a wicked person:

A wicked person's talk is prompted by sin in his heart; he sees no need to fear God. For it flatters and deceives him and, when his iniquity is found out, he does not change. Everything he says is mischievous and false; he has lost all understanding of right conduct; he lies in bed planning the mischief he will do. So set is he on his evil course that he rejects no wickedness. (Psalm 36:1–4)

Don't interpret God's promises to mean we won't run into problems or that we won't have to deal with distasteful outcomes. That's not what God has promised.

Most of our disappointment and pain fall into one of the following three categories, usually the first two:

1. A result of our failure to follow God's counsel, whether intentional or not.
2. A secondary result of other people failing to follow God's counsel; the terrible consequences they experience can spill over into the lives of those around them.
3. A catastrophic event, such as a natural disaster or illness.

We're all good at seeing someone else's mistakes. When we watch them go into a state of denial, playing the role of the victim, we scratch our heads and ask, "Why can't they see this picture? It's such an easy problem to fix!"

The choice a person makes will determine future consequences in his life. Rationalizing behavior that is contrary to God's counsel brings pain. Take a look at some verses found in Proverbs:

He who is wicked is caught in his own iniquities, held fast in the toils of his own sin; for want of discipline he will perish, wrapped in the shroud of his boundless folly. (Proverbs 5:22–23)

Someone still stubborn after much reproof will suddenly be broken past mending.... An evildoer is ensnared by his sin, but the doer of good will live and flourish." (Proverbs 29:1, 6)

Whoever refuses correction is his own worst enemy, but one who listens to reproof learns sense. Wisdom's

discipline is the fear of the LORD, and humility comes
before honour. (Proverbs 15:32-33)

The consequences described in Proverbs are certainly nothing to get
excited about. It's so easy to rationalize our behavior and, in the process,
make God irrelevant. Rationalizing inappropriate behavior always
means we're going to hurt the people around us. It's unavoidable.

The wicked boast of the desires they harbour; in their greed
they curse and revile the LORD. The wicked in their pride
do not seek God; there is no place for God in any of their
schemes. Their ways are always devious; your judgments are
beyond their grasp, and they scoff at all their adversaries....
He says to himself, 'God has forgotten; he has hidden his
face and seen nothing.' (Psalm 10:3–5, 11)

People both outside and inside the church are making these
unfortunate choices. It can include those dedicated to the Lord as
leaders in the church. They desire His blessings but refuse to accept
His counsel. God is not amused by the impact of their actions. The
following verses poignantly make this point. Notice, each verse is
addressing those who claim to know God.

God's word to a wicked person is this: What right have
you to recite my statutes, to take the words of my covenant
on your lips? For you hate correction and cast my words
out of your sight. (Psalm 50:16–17)

Her priests give rulings which violate my law, and profane
what is sacred to me. They do not distinguish between
sacred and profane, and enforce no distinction between
clean and unclean. They disregard my Sabbaths, and I am
dishonored among them...The common people resort to
oppression and robbery; they ill-treat the unfortunate
and the poor, they oppress the alien and deny him justice.
(Ezekiel 22:26, 29)

Peter speaks of the pain Lot suffered while living in Sodom and
Gomorrah. He writes, "Lot, a good man distressed by the dissolute
habits of the lawless society in which he lived; day after day every

sight and sound of their evil ways tortured that good man's heart" (2 Peter 2:7–8).

On the other hand, when we make a habit of identifying the changes that God would have us make in our lives, claim His promises of deliverance, and put His grace into action, positive things happen. We see God's hand at work in our life.

The first step in beginning this journey is asking God to give us insight into our lives so we can see ourselves as He sees us. The next step is to identify the areas in our lives that are causing problems and approach those who are enjoying the blessings we'd like to have. Ask yourself the following questions:

1. Do you know someone who took the time to learn and apply health concepts? For instance, is there someone who struggled with weight control and won?

2. Who do you know with a happy marriage? What's their secret? What can you learn from them to enhance your marriage? What changes do you need to make?

3. Are there families you know with well-disciplined children who respect their parents and value God in their lives? Listen to their counsel. What changes do you need to make?

4. Do you know people who have mastered the skills of financial management? Which of your attitudes regarding money need changing?

5. Do you know someone who has learned to balance their work life, their family time, and the time they spend with their church? What steps of faith will you need to make to regain balance in your life?

6. Perhaps you are working in a difficult environment. Do you know someone who has made dramatic changes resulting in blessings they never thought possible? What steps did they take? How did they prepare? How did they deal with the fear of the unknown?

It's when we just go through the motions, simply giving God lip service, that we ask the question, "Where is God, and how could He allow this to happen to me?" How hypocritical. We're the ones not treating God fairly! What's more, for each area in which we violate God's intention, we adversely affect all those within our sphere of influence.

All too often, we just want our own way; then, when events don't turn out right, we whine about the results. We don't really want to make any changes. As long as we insist on doing things our way, we will continue to look for ways to avoid the painful consequences of disobedience. Such lives are never settled. Isaiah 57:20–21 says, "But the wicked are like a storm-tossed sea, a sea that cannot be still, whose waters cast up mud and dirt. There is no peace for the wicked, says my God."

When we insist on doing things our way while praying to God for help, there's absolutely nothing He can do. We've tied His hands! Then we become frustrated that God's not answering our prayers, and our expectation that He will do something wonderful in our lives disappears. "The Lord's arm is not too short to save nor his ear too dull to hear; rather, it is your iniquities that raise a barrier between you and God; it is your sins that veil his face, so that he does not hear" (Isaiah 59:1–2).

What a terrible position for God to be in!

When I began to understand that God wanted to teach me His way in even the smallest things of life, He became a lot more relevant to me. It had a huge impact on my attitude and focus once I understood that God wants me to live life abundantly, but my sin gets in the way of His blessing me. It gave me a desire to understand and seek His counsel. I began to see that ignorance hurts both me and those around me. Jeremiah says, "When I came on your words I devoured them; they were joy and happiness to me, for you, Lord God of Hosts, have named me yours" (Jeremiah 15:16).

Ignorance is not bliss. Even when I make bad decisions out of ignorance, the outcome is still negative. Ignorance does not soften the impact of a poor choice.Consequently, my decision-making process changed. In the past, I avoided doing bad things only because I wanted to go to heaven. Now my choices came from a positive motivation. My focus shifted from a desire to go to heaven in the future to a desire to receive God's blessings now. This may sound too simple, but it's really what happened. Furthermore, I've seen a similar reaction in others.

When I speak with youth using this approach, their negativity disappears. God's promises, together with not wanting to miss a blessing, create a positive conversation. It enables them to make good decisions for the right reasons. They are doing things because it really will make their lives better. This approach brings simplicity. It opens the door for them to become seekers of the Word. Their imagination will be stretched as they begin to wonder what God has in store for them.

Another consequence of my changed attitude is a greater tolerance for others, even when they were making my life difficult. Don't get me wrong—I still strongly dislike some situations in which I find myself. However, I have a newfound patience when working with someone who is a major pain in my life. I'm acutely aware of the hurt they're experiencing, and I long to see their wounds healed. I see that the pain I cause others is no better than the pain they cause me.

Everything I do has a ripple effect. There are no exceptions. I'm not an island. My failure to follow God's counsel always brings disappointment and pain. Just as physical pain is a protective measure and a warning, emotional pain is too. It's a wake-up call, an opportunity to change course and make a positive difference.

My choices can limit the power of God. Despite the terrible effects of sin that I sometimes bring into other people's lives, He desires to work through me to heal and restore the lives of others. This is how God becomes relevant, through the combination of my personal experience and my reaching out a helping hand. Faith and prayer unleashes His power.

Let's look at a couple more examples. One of God's assurances to Israel through Moses was that there would never be any poor among them.

> "There will never be any poor among you if only you obey the LORD your God by carefully keeping these commandments which I lay upon you this day; for the LORD your God will bless you with great prosperity in the land which he is giving you to occupy as your holding" (Deuteronomy 15:4–5).

This verse is very direct; its meaning, clear. Yet, as you continue to read, God seems to say the direct opposite.

> When in any of your settlements in the land which the LORD your God is giving you one of your fellow-countrymen becomes poor, do not be hard-hearted or

close-fisted towards him in his need. Be open-handed towards him and lend him on pledge as much as he needs....Give freely to him and do not begrudge him your bounty, because it is for this very bounty that the LORD your God will bless you in everything that you do or undertake. The poor will always be with you in your land, and that is why I command you to be open-handed towards any of your countrymen there who are in poverty and need. (Deuteronomy 15:7–8, 10–11)

The seemingly contradictory passage is easily explained: God's blessings are for sharing. The promise is repeated in Proverbs: "He who gives to the poor will never want, but he who turns a blind eye gets nothing but curses" (Proverbs 28:27).

Yet generosity cannot be legislated. It must come from the heart by free choice. Greed, callousness, and legislative mandates always bring disastrous results. Just imagine how different our global economics would be if this counsel were followed! Just imagine, a system with inherent accountability. If someone is helping me with money or with life skills, I'm grateful for God's goodness and will naturally desire to do the same for someone else. This ripple effect creates a growing and sustainable demand for goods, which would minimize poverty and economic displacement. Government budgets would not be strained with social welfare expenditures, tax rates would be lower, and government waste would be minimized.

This counsel makes two assumptions: First, the community is embracing God's counsel; and second, bad things still happen in a sinful world. Things happen that are beyond our control. When bad things do happen, or when people grow up in less than optimal circumstances, the community steps in. Generosity balanced with accountability is the perfect recipe for a quick recovery.

This is such an important principle. When Israel lost sight of it, Ezekiel told Israel that their behavior was worse than that of Sodom and Gomorrah. When people believe that what they have has been earned by their own effort, the community is in trouble. When I've asked people what they think God was talking about in this passage, the answer I've always gotten is that Israel's homosexuality must have been even worse than Sodom and Gomorrah. Absolutely not! That's not even mentioned.

Did you not behave as they did and commit the same abominations? Indeed you surpassed them in depraved conduct. As I live, says the Lord GOD, your sister Sodom and her daughters never behaved as you and your daughters have done! This was the iniquity of your sister Sodom: she and her daughters had the pride that goes with food in plenty, comfort, and ease, yet **she never helped the poor in their need.**...It is you that must bear the humiliation, for your sins have pleaded your sisters' cause; your conduct is so much more abominable than theirs that they appear innocent in comparison. (Ezekiel 16:47–49, 52, emphasis supplied)

How much blunter can God be? Throughout Scripture, He repeats the promise of blessings to those who help the needy.

Happy is anyone who has a concern for the helpless! The LORD will save him in time of trouble; the LORD protects him and gives him life, making him secure in the land; the LORD never leaves him to the will of his enemies. (Psalm 41:1–2)

Whoever despises the hungry does wrong, but happy are they who are generous to the poor. (Proverbs 14:21)

Praise the LORD. Happy is he who fears the LORD, who finds deep delight in obeying his commandments....His house will be full of riches and wealth; his righteousness will stand sure forever....He lavishes his gifts on the needy; his righteousness will stand sure forever; in honour he carries his head high. (Psalm 112:1, 3, 9)

Rather, is not this the fast I require: to loose the fetters of injustice, to untie the knots of the yoke, and set free those who are oppressed, tearing off every yoke? Is it not sharing your food with the hungry, taking the homeless poor into your house, clothing the naked when you meet them, and never evading a duty to your kinsfolk? ...If you give of your own food to the hungry and satisfy the needs of the wretched, then light will rise for you out of darkness and dusk will be for you like noonday. (Isaiah 58:6–7, 10)

And it is in God's power to provide you with all good gifts in abundance, so that with every need always met to the full, you may have something to spare for every good cause; as scripture says: 'He lavishes his gifts on the needy; his benevolence lasts forever.' Now he who provides seed for sowing and bread for food will provide the seed for you to sow; he will multiply it and swell the harvest of your benevolence, and you will always be rich enough to be generous. Through our action such generosity will issue in thanksgiving to God, for as a piece of willing service this is not only a contribution towards the needs of God's people; more than that, it overflows in a flood of thanksgiving to God. (2 Corinthians 9:8–12)

The natural response to God's blessings is a desire to share. Christ dramatically makes this point in Matthew when He describes what will happen when He comes again to take His children home.

Then the king will say to those on his right, "You have my Father's blessing; come, take possession of the kingdom that has been ready for you since the world was made. For when I was hungry, you gave me food; when thirsty, you gave me drink; when I was a stranger, you took me into your home; when naked, you clothed me; when I was ill, you came to my help; when in prison, you visited me."... And the king will answer, "Truly I tell you: anything you did for one of my brothers here, however insignificant, you did for me." (Matthew 25:34–36, 40)

James drives home the same point. "A pure and faultless religion in the sight of God the Father is this: to look after orphans and widows in trouble and to keep oneself untarnished by the world" (James 1:27).

Simply put, God has given us an amazing abundance; we've barely scratched the surface in following God's counsel and receiving the blessings He desires to give. Worse yet, we take for granted the blessings we've received. Yet, many of us question God's power, love, and presence when we see the social ills that are a direct result of our failure to share the blessings He's given us. Once again, it's not God, but us! If we were aware of His blessings, if we knew His desire to bless us, if we simply trusted Him and opened our hands generously, we would create a ripple effect of God's awesome love.

Each of us has the power to demonstrate God's love and relevance in a world grown cynical about God's existence, let alone His love and willingness to make a difference in people's lives. Cynicism has flourished because of our failure to joyfully embrace His counsel. Paul writes, "As scripture says, 'Because of you the name of God is profaned among the Gentiles'" (Romans 2:24). Each of us has the choice of stepping out, experiencing His joy, and sharing His love in a world wracked with pain.

Earlier in this chapter, I listed catastrophic events as one of the major causes of disappointment and pain. How do we deal with a natural disaster that kills thousands, a child that dies of cancer, a loved one who dies in a fluke car accident, or a friend who suffers a violent death at another's hands? There are two examples in Scripture that come to mind. The first is the prophecy given by Jeremiah regarding the parents who would not be comforted over the death of their children. The second is John the Baptist's beheading by King Herod.

Matthew related the fulfillment of Jeremiah's prophecy in his gospel. He told about how an angel appeared to Joseph and told him to take baby Jesus and flee from King Herod to Egypt. Immediately afterward, King Herod inflicted terrible carnage on all baby boys under the age of two.

> When Herod realized that the astrologers had tricked him he flew into a rage, and gave orders for the massacre of all the boys aged two years or under, in Bethlehem and throughout the whole district, in accordance with the time he had ascertained from the astrologers. So the words spoken through Jeremiah the prophet were fulfilled: 'A voice was heard in Rama, sobbing in bitter grief; it was Rachel weeping for her children, and refusing to be comforted, because they were no more.' (Matthew 2:16–18)

Verse 18 is a quote of Jeremiah 31:15, where Jeremiah goes on to say,

> "These are the words of the LORD to her: **Cease your weeping, shed no more tears; for there will be a reward for your toil**, and they will return from the enemy's land. There will be hope for your posterity; your children will return within their own borders" (Jeremiah 31:16–17, emphasis supplied)

These verses now take on additional meaning. It wasn't just family and friends who couldn't console them; they were also refusing to be consoled by our heavenly Father! They had stopped trusting Him. They refused to believe that He was still present, to remember what He'd done in the past, and to hold on to His promises. In short, they felt that they'd been forgotten. His comfort wasn't accepted.

What might this toil be? It's the everyday challenges of life. This includes the challenges of earning a living, dealing with dishonest people, and dealing with suffering that comes from loss. God doesn't promise to insulate us from the effects of sin. However, he does promise to provide, heal, protect, and guide us. Jesus told his disciples, "'I have told you all this so that in me you may find peace. In the world you will have suffering. But take heart! I have conquered the world'" (John 16:33).

Jeremiah reassures them of God's feelings for Israel:

> "My heart yearns for him; I am filled with tenderness towards him. This is the word of the LORD.... Just as a loincloth is bound close to a man's body, so I bound all Israel and all Judah to myself, says the LORD, so that they should become my people to be a source of renown and praise and glory to me" (Jeremiah 31:20; 13:11).

It's certainly understandable that our emotions should overwhelm us when something terrible happens. The question is, Will we allow the Lord to comfort us?

Notice the intensity of David's emotions in the following passage. Notice how he, too, questions God's presence.

In the day of my distress I sought the Lord, and by night I lifted my hands in prayer. My tears ran unceasingly, I refused all comfort....'Will the Lord always reject me and never again show favour? Has his love now failed utterly? Will his promise never be fulfilled? Has God forgotten to be gracious? Has he in anger withheld his compassion? Has his right hand grown weak?' I said, 'Has the right hand of the Most High changed?' (Psalm 77:2, 7)

The very first step David takes is to remember. He looks to the past and remembers what God has done. He recalls God's faithfulness. By its very nature, despair means that we've come to believe we're all alone, that no one has ever experienced what we're going through. As an act of faith, David looks back.

"I call to mind the deeds of the LORD; I recall your wonderful acts of old; I reflect on all your works and consider what you have done. Your way, God, is holy; what god is as great as our God? You are a God who works miracles; you have shown the nations your power" (Psalm 77:11–14).

Once we remember, we can now reach forward and claim His promise of healing. Notice the healing that God brings:

LORD my God, **I cried to you and you healed me....** **You have turned my laments into dancing**; **you** have stripped off my sackcloth and **clothed me with joy**, that I may sing psalms to you without ceasing. LORD my God, I shall praise you forever. (Psalm 30:2, 11–12, emphasis supplied)

I am afflicted and in pain; **let your saving power, God, set me securely on high.**I shall praise God's name in song and glorify him with thanksgiving; that will please the LORD more than the offering of a bull, a young bull with horns and cloven hoofs. (Psalm 69:29–31, emphasis supplied)

When this is our experience, we demonstrate once again the power of God to transform us in spite of the scars that sin brings. A joyful heart in the face of adversity is a powerful testimony to the transformational power of God's grace.

This is in stark contrast to the person who spends life mourning, bitter over some injustice. Putting up with the pain of sin is the toil that Jeremiah is referring to when he says, "there will be a reward for your toil." This wasn't a part of God's plan. It's been imposed on God and us. Our eventual reward is heaven. Heaven has become a joyful hope that looks sweeter and sweeter every day as we let Jesus transform our lives. Going to heaven is now a positive motivation, not one rooted in fear. It's a day we hope for and anticipate. It's a day that can't come too soon. What a big difference!

John the Baptist is the second example of how to deal with catastrophic events. Let's start with a little background. After he preached about the coming Messiah and called hearers to make a change in their lives, John sat alone in prison, becoming increasingly discouraged. He began to question Jesus' ministry. Finally, he worked up the courage to have his disciples approach Jesus and ask if he was, in fact, the Messiah.

Certainly, John could have been freed in the same miraculous way that Peter and Paul were freed from prison. But, once again, John is called to trust that God's purpose is being best served through his situation. In responding to John's disciples, Jesus says little. Instead he chooses to act.

> There and then he healed many sufferers from diseases, plagues, and evil spirits; and on many blind people he bestowed sight. Then he gave them this answer: 'Go tell John what you have seen and heard: the blind regain their sight, the lame walk, lepers are made clean, the deaf hear, the dead are raised to life, the poor are brought good news – and happy is he who does not find me an obstacle to faith.' (Luke 7:21–23)

He elevates the importance of John's ministry—and, ultimately, yours and mine—when He says, "'I tell you, among all who have been born, no one has been greater than John; yet the least in the kingdom of God is greater than he is'" (v. 28).

The beautiful simplicity of Jesus' message is clear. John had successfully prepared the hearts of his hearers to understand, accept, and be transformed by the message of Immanuel, "God with us." Yet, God views our positive impact on those around us as of even greater importance!

Fulfilling this purpose will bring us joy that all the negative effects of sin can never take away. Only those who have experienced such joy understand this seemingly backwards way of thinking. Suddenly death is simply not the issue it is for others. Not only do we believe we're going to heaven, but the transformational power of grace brings peace—a peace based on the experience of knowing that God always keeps His promises and exceeds our expectations. Our minds are at rest knowing that, as always, all is well. This is what Christ meant when He told His disciples, "'I have told you all this so that in me you may find peace. **In the world you will have suffering. But take heart! I have conquered the world**'" (John 16:33, emphasis supplied).

God has not given us the option of living a life of fear!

Action Steps

1. Identify a few of your problems. Begin discovering the counsel that God has for each situation. Do you know people who haven't experienced these problems? Ask them for advice. Our situations are much more similar than we'd like to think.

2. Small changes can make a big difference. Begin making changes by taking little steps.

3. Begin making decisions because you don't want to miss out on the blessings God desires for you to enjoy. Teach this way of thinking to your children.

4. What impact has this change made on your view of God and your compassion for others?

5. Begin praying for others. Claim God's promises for wisdom and to see opportunities to help others. Ask God to demonstrate His power in their lives and to protect them from Satan.

Additional Scripture for Study

Exodus 14:14–15
John 14:1, 27
Joshua 1:6–9
Isaiah 49:14–16
Isaiah 50:4–9
Isaiah 51:7–13
Proverbs 10:24–25
Proverbs 13:18–19
Proverbs 15:6, 12, 22
Isaiah 5:18–21
Jeremiah 4:2-4

Chapter 7

A Sense of Community

Hidden Gem:

May they all be one; as you, Father, are in me, and I in you, so also may they be in us, that the world may believe that you sent me. (John 17:21)

About a year ago, I shared a very rough draft of this manuscript with a young couple. As the wife began reading and saw my excitement over the book of Deuteronomy, she asked if I'd study with them. It took us a full year to study thirty-four chapters. By the time we finished, they had become like family, their relationship with God had been transformed, and our study group had grown to over twenty-five people.

As they went through the book, they saw what God likes to do in people's lives now. Instead of engaging in arguments about doctrine with people, they were talking about what God had done in their lives; people were attracted to that. Originally, the husband joined the church to make his wife happy. Now he has become one of the leaders of his church, which he had attended inconsistently before this. Most of the new people in the Bible study have come as a result of this couple's contagious enthusiasm.

The group has become a wonderful place to share what's happening in our lives. It's a place to communicate life's challenges and get much-needed encouragement. Members share what God has done for them, scriptures they have discovered, and answers to prayer. When people have a correct view of God, it's a transforming experience. "Therefore encourage one another, build one another other up—as indeed you do" (1 Thessalonians 5:11).

By the unity shown among the community of believers, the world will be convinced that God sent Jesus, His Son. Christ creates a high standard of achievement, placing the responsibility on our shoulders. We will experience the same emotional and spiritual intimacy within the community of believers as Jesus and our heavenly Father enjoy. Despite all the distractions, we can and must experience the joy of intimacy.

This is another compelling reason for God's relevance in our lives. Intimacy is something people want, but few experience. There are so many forces at work that make it difficult for us to achieve it. Some of these forces are the demands of our jobs, our varying goals, cultural differences, and the isolation that can occur from using video games, the internet, and television.

Christ didn't say that, once we make it to heaven, we'll experience unity. Unity is to begin now. It is the standard of measurement that convinces the unbeliever that Jesus really is the Son of God who came, died, was resurrected, and stands at the right hand of our loving heavenly Father answering our prayers. As the transforming power of God's grace changes our lives, a spirit of unity is created in the home and community of believers.

Let's take a quick inventory of what an active faith brings to our lives:

1. **We experience God's joy and blessings as a result of His counsel.** We cannot sacrifice for God.

2. **We assume full responsibility for our actions.** We stop making excuses and blaming others for our painful outcomes. We understand sin as anything that prevents us from receiving the blessings He intends for our lives. As a result, we want to identify the sin. It causes us to look at the pain in our lives and ask, "What do I need to do differently? Who do I know that doesn't have this problem? I think I'll ask them for advice." We're not offended when we're shown our mistakes. It's something else to be thankful for—another opportunity to experience God's transforming grace!

3. **We become interested in learning to know His voice**. As we make our requests known, we rejoice over the doors He opens, knowing they are always for our benefit. This provides us with the necessary guidance to make sound decisions.

4. **We are eager to discover and claim God's promises and follow His counsel**. These assist us with life's challenges, giving us hope, guidance, deliverance, and wisdom.

5. **We are grateful for what He's already done and promises to do in the future**. Sharing His goodness happens spontaneously.

6. **As a result of our gratitude for what God has done, we have a spirit of empathy for others and a desire to serve.** We no longer see service as what we're supposed to do but as a pleasure. Because God's been so generous to us, we want to share the blessings. Sharing can include donations, personal experiences, and expertise. With each touch, we share God's blessing. We'll never know the breadth of its impact.

When these six elements are integrated into a community of believers, the impact is dramatic. We can't force them to happen. It's a natural, spontaneous outcome among a group of believers being transformed by the Holy Spirit.

Let's touch on a few of these outcomes. I'll also include a few anecdotes.

1. **As the community sees God's promises come true, it creates an excitement that encourages sharing and a desire to pray with and for others.**

2. **When the community prays and shares together, it encourages an atmosphere of acceptance, patience, and openness.**

3. **As the community becomes more accepting and open, people share their needs and day-to-day challenges.** This transformation is exciting to witness. We learn there's nothing to be gained by keeping our problems hidden. Hiding problems drags out the pain. The closer

we become to someone, the less we worry what he or she thinks of us. We already know! It's comforting that we can call and ask to be included in their prayers. At first we might worry that information shared in confidence will be inappropriately shared with others. However, the promise of healing more than offsets the potential risk. It's a wonderful boost in spirit to have someone call, ask how we're doing, and realize they really do want to know. Instead of giving them the usual, "Fine," we feel comfortable telling them what's happening in our lives. Hearing a friend's perspective and words of encouragement, supported by God's promises, helps keep us on track. We become increasingly aware of when our mental attitude strays. The blessing of friendship grows in value.

A member of our weekly Bible study group would sit in his car, waiting for the meeting to be almost over, before he would come in. He was afraid. After he began to form ties with those in the group, he started to come earlier. Once he took the risk and began attending our study group, I watched him transform from a withdrawn, uncommunicative, and gruff personality to an outspoken, warm, and gregarious individual. The change has been exciting to watch. Now when he walks in the room, he hugs members of the class. Sometimes this even includes visitors! Part of this transformation came about because of his involvement in a healthy community.

This man operates two trucks in British Columbia. The weakening U.S. dollar, the temporary drop in oil prices, and the reduction in construction caused a significant decrease in goods transported, which affected his income. He had recently purchased a brand new semi whose engine was made by Caterpillar. From the day he drove the truck off the lot, he had nothing but problems. It spent over 100 days in the shop for repairs. Of course, he was still responsible for making truck payments. With the loss in revenues, he fell behind on his loan payments, and his stress level soared. Ultimately, he was hospitalized for high blood pressure.

He shared his problem in our Bible study group. Afterward, I reviewed the situation with him and helped him write a letter to the president of Caterpillar. One month later, Caterpillar had not only repaired the truck, but had also paid an amount equaling four loan payments. Words can't describe how happy he was for my unanticipated help. I spent no more than forty-five minutes writing the letter, and approximately two hours reviewing his business plan to give him pointers on making decisions that would be critical for his business. For me, this was no big deal; but for my friend, it was huge! When I shared my talent and time, he opened up and began sharing other personal problems that he had been struggling with for years. Turning to Scripture to find answers to real problems increased his desire for a closer relationship with God. He eagerly accepted my offer to pray for him. A bond has been built between him and the members of our Bible study group. It's been a wonderful experience.

4. **As we become aware of people's problems, we feel a greater need to serve and to pray.** People's needs become apparent, and we discover opportunities to help. Our gratitude to God creates a desire to serve. It's easier to take time to give when we know we're not fighting life's challenges alone. This is why opportunities to serve become more apparent. Our hesitancy to serve disappears because we want others to experience His power in their lives. When we are focusing on serving others, we become more aware of the need for God's intervention. This creates a need to pray together for God's guidance and blessings. Our prayers will have more urgency; the requests will broaden and become less routine.

As we discover and use His promises, His answers are clear, and our excitement grows. Jesus tells us in Matthew, "'And again I tell you: if two of you agree on earth about any request you have to make, that request will be granted by my heavenly Father. For where two or three meet together in my name, I am there among them'" (Matthew 18:19–20).

James takes Jesus' words and puts them to practical use. "Therefore confess your sins to one another, and pray for one another, that you may be healed. A good man's prayer is very powerful and effective. Elijah was a man just like us; yet when he prayed fervently that there should be no rain, the land had no rain for three and a half years" (James 5:16-17). There's power in praying together for the needs of the community.

5. **Active sharing, serving, and praying create emotional bonds that bring encouragement and rest.** I look forward to spending time with friends who I know will give me wise advice that sees to my best interests. It brings such a relief. David says, "How good and how pleasant it is to live together as brothers in unity.... It is as if the dew of Hermon were falling on the mountains of Zion. There the Lord bestows his blessing, life forevermore" (Psalm 133:1, 3). Jesus told Simon to encourage his fellow disciples. "'Simon, Simon, take heed: Satan has been given leave to sift all of you like wheat; but I have prayed for you, Simon, that your faith may not fail; and when you are restored, give strength to your brothers'" (Luke 22:31–32).

6. **Active sharing, service.and prayer create emotional bonds that improve the health of each member of the community.** Studies have shown that achieving intimacy improves our overall health. One of my favorite examples is in the book, *Outliers* by Malcolm Gladwell. In the introduction, Mr. Gladwell shares the extensive research performed by a physician and a sociologist in the mid-fifties in the community of Roseto, Pennsylvania. What caught them by surprise was that no one from the community was dying from any of the normal diseases of affluence. They were simply dying of old age! The sociologist, John Bruhn, shared with Mr. Gladwell: "There was no suicide, no alcoholism, no drug addiction, and very little crime. They didn't have anyone on welfare. Then we looked at peptic ulcers. They didn't have any of those either. These people were dying of old age. That's it." (*Outliers,* p. 7)

Upon investigating the health habits of the town, they found that 41 percent of a typical Rosetan's diet was from fat! They didn't exercise, and they smoked heavily. They next investigated their genetics and learned that Rosetans lived longer than their cousins in both other parts of the United States and in Italy. When they checked to see if there was a geographical or environmental effect, they found that those in the surrounding communities had death rates from heart disease at three times the rate of those in Roseto.

They also found that this community had an extremely tight social structure. The elderly felt respected and had a sense of belonging, several generations lived together, and there were twenty-two separate civic organizations in a town of only two thousand people. In Roseto, they found a culture that discouraged the wealthy from flaunting their wealth and protected the dignity of those struggling financially.

Absolutely amazing! Yet, we shouldn't be amazed. As we've seen, the promises repeatedly given to Moses were that, if we follow God's counsel, we'd prosper and be successful in all that we do. Christ repeated the promise when he said, "I have come that they may have life, and may have it in all its fullness" (John 10:10).

The truly amazing part is that experiences such as this aren't standard among God's people. This shouldn't be seen as outside the norm! The fact that it is, demonstrates just how much we've failed to grasp the relevance of following God's counsel in our daily lives.

If the words "prosper" and "successful" trouble you, take a look at the words God gave to both Moses and Ezekiel. Moses says:

> I summon heaven and earth to witness against you this day: I offer you the choice of life or death, blessing or curse. **Choose life** and you and your descendants will live; love the LORD your God, **obey him, and hold fast to him: that is life for you and length of days on the soil**

> which the LORD swore to give to your forefathers, Abraham, Isaac, and Jacob." (Deuteronomy 30:19–20, emphasis supplied)

In Ezekiel 20:11, 13, and 21, the Lord reminds Ezekiel that He gave Israel His laws so that they might have life. He wasn't speaking of eternal life. There is no way this can be interpreted to mean a future promise. He was clearly talking about their present dismal condition. Hosea provides the following beautiful illustration:

> I shall be as dew to Israel that they may flower like the lily, strike root like the poplar, and put out fresh shoots, that they may be as fair as the olive and fragrant as Lebanon.... I am the pine tree that shelters you; your prosperity comes from me.... Let the wise consider these things and let the prudent acknowledge them: the LORD's ways are straight and the righteous walk in them, while sinners stumble. (Hosea 14:5–6, 8–9)

When the above characteristics are absent, what happens to a community? One problem is the individual's inability to discern that he has a problem. He erroneously believes that his problems are someone else's fault. He refuses to accept responsibility for his actions. This reflects the litigious environment in North America. Scripture describes this situation:

> 'Because they did not accept my counsel and spurned all my reproof, now they will eat the fruits of their conduct and have a surfeit of their own devices; for simpletons who turn a deaf ear come to grief, and the stupid are ruined by their own complacency. But whoever listens to me will live without a care, undisturbed by fear of misfortune.' (Proverbs 1:30–33)

> The way of the wicked is like deep darkness, and they do not know what has been their downfall. (Proverbs 4:19)

> He who is wicked is caught in his own iniquities, held fast in the toils of his own sin; for want of discipline he

will perish, wrapped in the shroud of his boundless folly.
(Proverbs 5:22–23)

The Lord spoke to Ezekiel and told him to make the inhabitants of Jerusalem see their abominable conduct. Finally, in Chapter 20, the elders of Israel came to consult the Lord, but Ezekiel said the Lord wouldn't allow them to consult Him because they had refused to listen to His words. God reminded them, "'I brought them out of Egypt and led them into the wilderness. There I gave my statutes to them and taught them my laws; **it is by keeping them that mortals have life**" (vv. 10–11). The Lord was talking about their quality of life.

Let's look at two examples that contrast two communities—one that follows God's counsel and one that rejects it.

When God brought the Israelites out of Egypt, a dramatic change in culture was required. Moses said, "You are not to act as we act here today, everyone doing as he pleases" (Deuteronomy 12:8). Repeated instances of disobedience required God to deal sternly with Israel, outlining laws that included swift punishment for violators. This was absolutely necessary if there was to be any chance of creating a model community that would be the envy of the surrounding nations. Reversing the lawless dynamics required a strong personality to establish and consistently apply the rule of law. Clear consequences had to be spelled out. When someone tested the boundaries, they had to learn that the rules would be objectively enforced in order for the situation to improve.

During the years immediately following the death of Moses and Joshua, God's plan was carried out. However, the blessings associated with God's laws were soon forgotten, and anarchy reappeared.

God gave Israel a promise in Deuteronomy: if they followed His commandments and statutes, the surrounding nations would admire them and God. Unfortunately, they didn't like the idea of being different, so they followed the same dysfunctional ways of the surrounding nations. Over the years, their situation went from bad to worse.

The book of Judges tracks the ongoing deterioration of their community. Finally, we read of a horrific story in Judges 17 to 21. Forty-eight thousand men from the tribe of Benjamin were killed, along with virtually all the Benjamite women and children. The entire tribe was wiped out because they decided to defend a small group of men who raped and beat a woman to death. In Judges 17:6 and Judges 21:25, the phrase is repeated, "Everyone did what was right in his own eyes." There was no one among the Benjamites that would stand up for the rule of law.

Interestingly, this is the same approach used by Satan when he tempted Eve. "'For God knows that, as soon as you eat it, your eyes will be opened and you will be like God himself, knowing both good and evil'" (Genesis 3:5).

Whenever we create our own standard of right or wrong, we lose the ability to hold ourselves accountable. We can't see that we've gone off track. Whenever we sidestep God's counsel, pain and suffering is the guaranteed result. Then, when we see the bad outcomes, we turn to our own, flawed solutions. For instance, once the Israelites reached the bottom of their immoral pit, they erroneously followed the example of the surrounding nations and sought a king, thinking that would get them on the right track.

When God's spirit is absent, the environment is marked by disorder. People are insistent on doing things their own way, and they resort to force to impose their way on others. Reasoning, integrity, and empathy disappear. It's every man for himself. Win-win solutions become nonexistent, and humility is seen as a weakness. No independent standard is used to differentiate between right and wrong. There can be no self-control or accountability in these kinds of situations. Experiencing the blessing of intimacy is impossible!

In sharp contrast is the story of the healing and joy that Israel experienced during the reign of King Hezekiah. These astounding proceedings are recorded in 2 Chronicles 29–31. I've identified the following key events:

1. **Hezekiah Calls the Levites to Repentance and Reformation** (2 Chronicles 29:3–17)

   King Hezekiah repairs the doors of the temple and calls together the Levite priests. He assumes responsibility for Israel's unfaithfulness and calls the Levites to set things right with God. He commands them to restore the temple, recommit themselves to the Lord's service, and complete the sacrificial offerings for all of Israel.

2. **Everyone Praises God** (2 Chronicles 29:25–30)

   As directed years earlier by King David, both during and following the sacrifices, King Hezekiah, his officers, and all of the Levites joyfully praised the Lord by singing songs and playing trumpets, lutes, lyres, and cymbals.

3. **Hezekiah Calls Israel to Commit themselves to the Lord and Seek His Guidance** (2 Chronicles 30:1–20)

   King Hezekiah calls all of Judah and Israel to observe Passover. He challenges them to recommit their lives to the Lord and seek His guidance. Many refused to come, reacting to King Hezekiah's call with scorn and ridicule. But the positive response was overwhelming. Amazingly, this was the largest observance of Passover ever! There were so many people that they couldn't complete the required sacrifice. King Hezekiah prays, "'May the good LORD grant pardon to everyone who makes a practice of seeking guidance of God, the LORD the God of his forefathers, even if he has not observed the rules of purification for the sanctuary.' The LORD heard Hezekiah and healed the people." (vv. 18–20)

4. **Israel Celebrates with Unrestrained Joy** (2 Chronicles 30:21–27)

   The people's confession and commitment frees God to heal them. They are so overjoyed that they praise God with unrestrained fervor and extend the Feast of Unleavened Bread for an additional seven days!

   "There was great rejoicing in Jerusalem, the like of which had not been known there since the days of Solomon son of David king of Israel. The priests and the Levites stood to bless the people, and their voice was heard when their prayer reached God's holy dwelling-place in heaven" (vv. 26–27).

5. **Israel Gives Generously** (2Chronicles 31:3–10)

   King Hezekiah is filled with such joy and gratitude that he makes a generous donation to the temple. As outlined in Deuteronomy 26, he also commands the people in Jerusalem to make a donation to the priests so they can devote themselves to the law of God. The people donated generously from the first fruits of their grain, new wine, oil, honey, and produce of their land. They also brought a full tithe of everything.The people living in the countryside also gave generously. They gave so much that the produce was stacked in heaps!

6. **Israel Enjoys Prosperity** (2 Chronicles 31:8–10, 21)
   When Hezekiah and his officers came and saw the heaps, they praised the LORD and his people Israel. Hezekiah consulted the priests and the Levites about these heaps, and Azariah the chief priest, who was of the line of Zadok answered, 'From the time when the people began to bring their contribution into the house of the LORD, they have had enough to eat, enough and to spare; indeed, the LORD has so greatly blessed them that they have this great store left over.'

Here's another little gem. Their prosperity was the fulfillment of another one of God's promises.

"The LORD has recognized you this day as his special possession, as he promised you, and you are to keep all his commandments; high above all the nations which he has made he will raise you, to bring him praise and fame and glory, and to be a people holy to the LORD your God, according to his promise" (Deuteronomy 26:18–19).

The reign of King Hezekiah is summarized this way: "**Whatever he undertook in the service of the house of God and in obedience to the law and the commandment to seek guidance of his God, he did with all his heart, and he prospered**" (2 Chronicles 31:21,emphasis supplied)

I would love to be part of such a vibrant, healthy community!

Notice, there's also accountability within the community. What if Hezekiah hadn't called on the priests to renew their commitment? What if he hadn't called on the community to prepare for and celebrate Passover? No one was forced to celebrate; however, those who responded to the call understood what was expected of them. They understood King Hezekiah's focus on restoration. For the Israelites who responded to the king's call of renewal, his prayer of mercy was immediately answered; all were healed.

A strong community also has strong leaders. Strength, mercy, accountability, and love are integrated. We frequently get confused about this within the church community. It doesn't work to turn a blind eye to problems, hoping for an eventual change of heart. Harsh and condemning tones won't bring restoration either. A call for renewal and restoration needs to be more than an altar call. There are blessings to claim today that will otherwise be forfeited forever. A future change in heart will bring future blessings; however, missed opportunities for renewal are blessings forever lost.

The steps necessary to create this experience are always the same. There are no cultural or economic constraints. This is why Jesus uses unity as the measure of Christian authenticity and relevance. Who wouldn't want to be a part of this kind of a community?

When we joyfully accept God's law as our standard of behavior, accept responsibility for our actions, seek His guidance, and accept the grace given through Jesus Christ, there will always be a transformation. God's spirit of joy, peace, and gratitude naturally builds a spirit of unity and intimacy. It brings joy! On the other hand, if we decide what the standard of behavior should be, we can expect a train wreck in our relationships, resulting in loneliness and discouragement. It really is just that simple.

There's only one question to be asked, the same question I have asked repeatedly: "When are we going to take God's word to heart and begin enjoying the life He intended for His children?" It is only when we choose to follow His counsel, accept His grace, and claim His promises that we will indisputably demonstrate that Jesus Christ is truly the Son of God who came to take away the sins of the world so that we can live an abundant life.

Action Steps

1. Set a goal to introduce yourself to people at church you don't know. Jesus methodically reached out to people He didn't know. Being a friend is a ministry.

2. Seek to help someone who has a need.

3. Identify how these individuals might help you grow. Identify how you might help them grow.

4. Instead of complaining about what's not right at church, decide what you will consistently do to encourage others. Make it your passion and not a job!

5. Ask someone if you can pray for her; be prepared to give her your prayer request.

6. Each week, be prepared to share what God's done for you during the week.

Scripture for Additional Study

1. 1 John 3:16–17; 5:14–17

2. Leviticus 19:17–18

3. Luke 17:3–4

4. Galatians 6:1–2, 9–10

5. 2 Timothy 3:1–7

6. 1 Thessalonians 5:11–18

7. Ephesians 4:1–7

8. Matthew 28:18–20

9. Luke 14:12–14

Chapter 8

The Forgotten Gem

Hidden
Gem:

As the new heavens and the new earth which I am making will endure before me, says the LORD, so will your posterity and your name endure. Month after month at the new moon, week after week on the Sabbath, all mankind will come to bow before me, says the LORD. (Isaiah 66:22–23)

A couple of weeks ago, my neighbor and I were reflecting about how we both are a bit too cerebral and task driven. At the beginning of each day, we've got a list of things left over from the day before, plus new tasks that need completing. We desire God to direct our lives; however, we find ourselves struggling to slow down our "processors" so we can hear God's still quiet voice. I never feel good that I'm squeezing in thirty to sixty minutes each day to spend time with God.

It's not just God whom I squeeze in. I also squeeze in inadequate time with my wife and three children. I'm dissatisfied with all the squeezing I do. I find that as I squeeze, I forget. I forget past lessons that I've learned, the contributions others have made in my life, and the many blessings that surround me.

I thank God for this hidden gem of the Sabbath, a time of rest God has made just for me. I pray that, by the time you've reached this chapter, you've found a new frame of reference that has brought new found joy to your life. It's quite remarkable to me that, by just a few seemingly minor adjustments in our perspective, Scripture takes on an entirely new and exciting meaning. Out of habit, I now view every command as an invitation to a special blessing from our heavenly Father. My life is now filled with positive choices, and I'm looking forward to the day that I will no longer have to put up with Satan's temptations.

Christ's death and resurrection was the fulfillment of God's promise of restoration. As Paul so succinctly said, "I speak God's hidden wisdom, his secret purpose framed from the very beginning to bring us to our destined glory" (1 Corinthians 2:7). God has begun the eternal process of transforming me into His image day by day. He didn't wait for the cross to get the process started for humanity. Instead, restoration began the moment Adam and Eve renewed their commitment and sought God's guidance. They looked forward with hope to the coming Messiah.

If God had waited for Jesus' death and resurrection, He couldn't have brought Enoch, Moses, or Elijah to heaven. God's close friendship with them was confirmation that the restoration process had already begun. He wasn't going to wait until the cross to begin enjoying eternal fellowship with man. He has always visualized the wonderful relationship we can have with Him. We were the ones who couldn't see the joy of fellowship with our Creator. Yet our failure to see this vision didn't tie His hands.

Reaching out to people assaulted by Satan and damaged by sin has created unique challenges for God. We're forgetful, our natural focus is on ensuring our own survival, and we're not good listeners. Consequently, we struggle to slow down and hear his voice, to accept and claim His promises, and to remember the marvelous works He's done for us in the past and will do in the future.

God has given us another hidden gem to help us remember Him and deepen our fellowship with our Creator, Deliverer, and Transformer. It's called the Sabbath. It was established at creation and repeated to Israel at Mt. Sinai in the fourth commandment. Like all the other commandments, the Sabbath has been a tremendous blessing for my family and me.

Our ability to keep growing in faith depends on remembering what the Lord has done in our past. By remembering, our awe of God stays fresh. Our reinvigorated faith gives us new experiences for which to praise Him and for sharing with others. Our witness stays vibrant.

When God delivered Israel, He frequently told them to remember. Let's look at a few examples.

➢ When the Lord brought Israel out of slavery from Egypt, He told them to remember that momentous event by observing the Feast of Unleavened Bread. "You must have the record of it as a sign upon your hand, and a reminder on your forehead to make sure that the law of the LORD is always on your lips, because the LORD with a strong hand brought you out of Egypt" (Exodus 13:9).

➢ When Israel defeated the Amalakites by upholding Moses' arms, the Lord told Moses to record it. "Moses built an altar, and named it 'The LORD is my Banner'" (Exodus 17:15).

➢ When Israel crossed the Jordon River, Joshua took twelve stones and told Israel,

> "'In days to come, when your descendants ask their fathers what these stones mean, you are to explain to them that Israel crossed this Jordan on dry land, for the LORD your God dried up the waters of the Jordan in front of you until you had gone across, just as the LORD your God did at the Red Sea when he dried it up for us until we had crossed. **Thus all people on earth will know how strong is the hand of the LORD; and thus you will always stand in awe of the LORD your God**" (Joshua 4:21–24, emphasis supplied).

➢ Jesus, too, understood the importance of remembering. When He was washing the disciples' feet and celebrating His final Passover before His crucifixion, He told them to repeat His example.

> "Then if I, your Lord and Teacher, have washed your feet, you also ought to wash one another's feet. I have set you an example: you are to do as I have done for you. In very truth I tell you,

a servant is not greater than his master, nor a messenger than the one who sent him. If you know this, happy are you if you act upon it" (John 13:14–17).

Psalm 78 provides a summary of Israel's relationship with God. This Psalm is referencing Deuteronomy 34:11–12. Beginning with Jacob, it tells us that God had given them a "solemn charge and established a rule in Israel, which he commanded our forefathers to teach their descendants, so that it might be known to a future generation, to children yet to be born, and they in turn would repeat it to their children. They were charged to put their trust in God, to hold his great acts ever in mind and to keep his commandments" (Psalm 78:5–7). Tragically, it says, "They had not kept God's covenant; they had refused to live by his law; they forgot the things he had done, the wonders he had shown them" (vv. 10–11). The reference to their forgetfulness and failure to trust the Lord is repeated four times:

- "They forgot the things he had done, the wonders he had shown them" (v. 11).
- "When the LORD heard this, he was infuriated: fire raged against Jacob, anger blazed up against Israel, because they put no faith in God, no trust in his power to save" (vv. 21–22).
- "In spite of all, they persisted in their sin and had no faith in his wonders" (v. 32).
- "They did not keep in mind his power or the day when he delivered them from the enemy" (v. 42).

In Hebrews 3:7-11, we are warned to not repeat the same mistake.

'Today', therefore, as the Holy Spirit says—Today if you hear his voice, do not grow stubborn as in the rebellion, at the time of testing in the desert, where your forefathers tried me and tested me, though for forty years they saw the things I did. Therefore I was incensed with that generation and said, Their hearts are forever astray; they would not discern my ways; so I vowed in my anger, **they shall never enter my rest.**" (emphasis supplied)

Every time Israel challenged God, the issue was always trust. They challenged God about the guidance He gave Moses and over food and water. God angrily told Moses, "Ten times they have challenged me and not obeyed my voice" (Numbers 14:23). Each time they thought they had a problem, they forgot what God had done in the past. They didn't believe He was with them.

Remembering God's answers calms our fears so that we can step forward in faith, knowing He will once again guide and provide for our needs. Remembering is essential to our ability to trust God and claim the power of His grace.

If you are depending upon your own skills to survive in a hostile environment, how can you rest? God does not want us to be ravaged by stress and fear. Jesus said, "'Set your troubled hearts at rest. Trust in God always; trust also in me...Peace is my parting gift to you, my own peace, such as the world cannot give" (John 14:1, 27).

Paul describes those who have learned the lessons of trust, guidance and joyful obedience: "For all who are led by the Spirit of God are sons of God. The Spirit you have received is not a spirit of slavery, leading you back into a life of fear, but a Spirit of adoption, enabling us to cry 'Abba! Father!'" (Romans 8:14–15).

Did you catch that? We're led by the Spirit of God and called out of a life of fear! Here's that familiar theme again: When we trust Jesus to guide every aspect of our lives, there's no room for fear. This is our only way to rest in a world where every man, woman, and child is assaulted by Satan.

The core purpose of the Sabbath is to enable us to dwell in Him, celebrate His goodness, and experience His blessing of rest. It energizes us for the coming week.

In the last chapter, we saw that the people of Israel sank so low that they almost wiped out the tribe of Benjamin. In Judges, the cause of their problem is identified:

> When that whole generation was gathered to its forefathers, and was succeeded by another generation, **who did not acknowledge the Lord and did not know what he had done** for Israel, then the Israelites did what was wrong in the eyes of the Lord by serving the baalim. (Judges 2:10–11, emphasis supplied).

Notice that, when they forgot the Lord, they did what was wrong in His eyes. It's cause and effect. We also saw this in the story of King Hezekiah. Israel had totally forgotten the Lord, and the king called them to remember the great things He had done.

The fourth commandment begins with this in mind. He calls us to take time to *remember*: remember the great things he's done in the past; remember what He's done in our lives during the past week; remember how He's delivered us from difficult situations; and remember how He's shown us new sins and given us victory over them.

God presents His blueprint for our happiness, and we, as is our habit, act as if we know better. Whenever we disregard His plan, we're the ones who pay the consequences. We miss out on the blessing.

The fourth commandment is found in both Exodus and Deuteronomy. Let's first look at the reference in Exodus.

> Remember to keep the Sabbath day holy. You have six days to labour and do all your work; but the seventh day is a Sabbath of the LORD your God; that day you must not do any work, neither you, nor your son or your daughter, your slave or your slave-girl, your cattle, or the alien residing among you; **for in six days the LORD made the heavens and the earth, the sea, and all that is in them**, and **on the seventh day he rested**. Therefore the LORD blessed the Sabbath day and declared it holy. (Exodus 20:8–11, emphasis supplied)

In Deuteronomy, the commandment is slightly different.

> Observe the Sabbath day and keep it holy as the LORD your God commanded you. You have six days to labour and do all your work; but the seventh day there is a Sabbath of the LORD your God; that day you must not do any work, neither you, nor your son or your daughter, your slave or your slave-girl, your ox, your donkey, or any of your cattle, or the alien residing among you, so that your slaves and slave-girls may rest as you do. **Bear in mind that you were slaves in Egypt, and the LORD your God brought you out with a strong hand and an outstretched arm**, and **for that reason** the LORD

your God has commanded you to keep the Sabbath day.
(Deuteronomy 5:12–15, emphasis supplied)

Taken together, God commands us to observe the Sabbath for the following reasons:

1. To remember that He is the Creator of all things. God spoke and it was. Meditating on these realities can only boost our assurance that God is faithful and can be trusted. There's nothing too big for Him.

2. To remember that we serve a Creator who is all-powerful. On behalf of ourselves and those in our community, we are called to pray that

   "The God of peace, who brought back from the dead our Lord Jesus, the great Shepherd of the sheep, through the blood of an eternal covenant, make [us] perfect in all goodness so that [we] may do his will; and may he create in us what is pleasing to him, through Jesus Christ, to whom be glory for ever and ever! Amen" (Hebrews 13:20–21).

3. To remember that we serve a personal God. Just as He personally brought Israel out of Egypt and dwelt with them, He is interested in being directly involved in our lives. He didn't just create the world and then step out of the picture. He's our Father—a personal God who is right by our side at all times. He has a powerful arm and He uses it because He loves us and desires to bless us. He's also very much aware of the sin problem. By remembering this, we'll call on Him; and when we do, He's promised to answer. In short, He's willing to use that powerful arm again and again and again! This way God remains relevant and we stay in awe of Him. It bolsters our faith. We will claim His promises and His hand in our lives, which encourages other people to get to know Him. We become powerful outreach tools in His hands.

4. To remember that observing the Sabbath is active faith. It cannot become just a mental exercise. Unsolved problems, pressing tasks at work, preparation for school

exams, homework, and household chores are all put aside. We're giving God the opportunity to demonstrate that He provides for all of our needs. We're claiming His promised rest. It's focused celebration. Simply keeping it in mind is not enough. This demonstration of our faith serves as a powerful witness to our families, friends, and associates. When others see us remembering, it points them toward remembering too.

5.   To remember that God gave us a rest day to share. When God gave us the seventh-day to rest, He created a common timeframe for the community to get together and collectively celebrate, share, and encourage each other. He just made it easy for us to get our calendars in sync!

6.   To remember that everyone is called to rest. God doesn't just call us to rest. He calls everyone to rest; it doesn't matter if they have a personal relationship with our Lord. It even includes our animals—they deserve a rest too! All of us are given the same 24-hour period to take a break and recharge our batteries.

Observing the Sabbath isn't something we do for God. Instead, it's another powerful example of God providing a plan to protect and heal us. Remembering this ensures we won't view God as harsh, aloof, inflexible, or arbitrary. We won't lose sight of His never-ending love and compassion for us. This is what Christ meant when He said, "'The Sabbath was made for man, not man for the Sabbath'" (Mark 2:27).

As God so often does with His commands, He offers blessings for remembering the Sabbath, promises specifically tied to its celebration. These promises are not repeated for any other activity or any other day of observance. Scripture promises no such blessings when we shift the activities of Sabbath worship and celebration to Sunday. I guess that's an additional incentive so that we follow through and *remember*! We make the choice to rest on His day to receive the blessing He promised and to experience His glory.

"Say to the Israelites: Above all you must keep my Sabbaths, **for the Sabbath is a sign between me and you in every generation** that you may know that **I am the LORD who hallows you**" (Exodus 31:13, emphasis supplied). Here's another wonderful confirmation that God's grace has been working to protect us from sin, to transform us, and to restore His image in us. This reminds us that our God never changes.

> "The Israelites must keep the Sabbath, observing it in every generation as a covenant forever. It is a sign forever between me and the Israelites, for in six days the LORD made the heavens and the earth, but on the seventh day he ceased work and refreshed himself" (vv. 16–17).

The Sabbath is not just for Jews; it's for everyone. God explains:

> These are the words of the LORD: The eunuchs who keep my Sabbaths, who choose to do my will and hold fast to my covenant, will receive from me something better than sons and daughters, a memorial and a name in my own house and within my walls; I shall give them everlasting renown, an imperishable name. **So too with the foreigners who give their allegiance to me**, to minister to me and love my name and become my servants, all who keep the Sabbath unprofaned and hold fast to my covenant: **these I shall bring to my holy hill and give them joy in my house of prayer**. (Isaiah 56:4–7, emphasis supplied)

Isaiah also reminds us how to observe the Sabbath:

> If you refrain from Sabbath journeys and from doing business on my holy day, **if you call the Sabbath a day of joy** and the LORD's holy day worthy of honour, if you honour it **by desisting from work and not pursuing your own interests** or attending to your own affairs, then **you will find your joy in the LORD, and I shall make you ride on the heights of the earth, and the holding of your father Jacob will be yours to enjoy. The LORD himself has spoken**. (Isaiah 58:13–14, emphasis supplied)

It is very clear that Israel lost sight of the Sabbath blessing God gave them. The Lord reminds them,

> "I brought them out of Egypt and led them into the wilderness. There I have given my statutes to them and taught them my laws; it is by keeping them that mortals have life. Further, **I gave them my Sabbaths to serve as a sign between us**, so that they would know that **I am the LORD who sanctified them**." (Ezekiel 20:10–12, emphasis supplied)

Ever since I came to understand the blessing that God has in store for me, this twenty-four hour period that begins at Friday sundown and ends Saturday at sunset has become the high point of my week. God has given me these hours to put aside all the problems that I manage during the week. All household chores are put on hold. I look forward to enjoying a leisurely dinner with my wife and children. None of us are hurrying to prepare for the next day's events. We sit around the table enjoying each other's company, laughing, and sharing. These hours give my wife and I time to talk and share.

On Saturday (Sabbath) morning, we go to church, worship the Lord, and enjoy fellowshipping and studying the Bible with other believers. The afternoon is frequently spent visiting with others. In Hawaii, this included a picnic in a park, going for a walk, helping someone in need, or participating in a church activity. It's simply a wonderful time to enjoy visiting with those who are special to us and to hear what the Lord has done in their lives. This twenty-four hour period gives me just a little glimpse of what eternity will be like. The one missing element is that God is not yet dwelling with us in the same way He will in heaven. The Sabbath always ends too quickly.

Experiencing this blessing makes it is easier to remember all that the Lord has done in my life and to step out in faith. I just know that He wants to continue to enrich and bless me in ways that I have yet to understand. I could never give up this blessing. I am so thankful that God gave the Sabbath to help me remember that He's provided a way to heal the scars caused by sin; to develop intimate relationships with my heavenly Father, my wife, children, and brothers and sisters in Christ; and to reach out and serve others.

The Sabbath, like so many of the gifts given by our heavenly Father, has been tragically distorted. Consequently, His simplicity, loving kindness and compassion have been misinterpreted or forgotten.

He's asking, "Do you trust me, believing that I know what's best for your life?" God wants us to flourish, not just get by. He even guarantees it. God told Isaiah, "For my thoughts are not your thoughts, nor are your ways my ways....So is it with my word issuing from my mouth; it will not return to me empty without accomplishing my purpose and succeeding in the task for which I sent it" (Isaiah 55:8, 11).

The Sabbath is a blessing God knows we need to experience. Once we do, we will never turn back. We will even continue to celebrate it throughout eternity. (Isaiah 66:23–24)

There's nothing to sacrifice; just blessings to receive! "Taste and see that the LORD is good. Happy are they who find refuge in him!" (Psalm 34:8).

Action Steps

1. Sabbath is a dwelling experience; it's not about just attending church on a different day of the week. Ask God to bring someone into your experience that has joyfully embraced Sabbath.

2. Celebrating the Sabbath is an act of faith. Identify what changes you will need to make in your life to observe it. Remember the promises as you take the first steps. Ask your accountability partner to pray for and with you.

3. The Sabbath is a wonderful time for bonding by sharing with family and friends who also love Jesus. Identify activities that will do this. Put anything that gets in the way off to the side.

4. Relax and enjoy mealtime, and identify activities that you can do with your family to uplift someone who has special needs.

Additional Scripture for Study

1. Psalm 95:11
2. Hebrews 4:3–11
3. Psalm 78
4. Romans 8:12–16

Chapter 9

An Angry, Loving God

Jonathan Edwards, one of America's most prominent early preachers, characterizes God's anger in such vivid, horrific terms that we could easily draw the wrong conclusion that God is anxiously waiting to cast us into eternal hell. He writes, "God has laid himself under no obligation, by any promise to keep any natural man out of hell one moment" (from "Sinners in the Hands of an Angry God"). Further on he writes,

> He that holds you over the pit of hell, much as one holds a spider, or some loathsome insect over the fire, abhors you, and is dreadfully provoked: his wrath towards you burns like fire; he looks upon you as worthy of nothing else, but to be cast into the fire; he is of purer eyes than to bear to have you in his sight; you are ten thousand times more abominable in his eyes, that the most hateful venomous serpent is in ours.

There's nothing in this description of God that draws me to Him. I see only two viable outcomes of this perspective: either I'll want nothing to do with Him, or I'll come to church to avoid His dreaded punishment. Neither evokes the spirit of adoration, thankfulness, and joy which is necessary for real worship.

Scripture has given us a wonderful picture of a loving heavenly Father who never intended that we suffer the painful consequences of sin. Once sin entered the picture, He immediately put a plan in place to protect us, heal us, and restore us so we could reflect His image.

Clearly, our picture of God's anger is incomplete and distorted. As we might expect, Satan promotes this distorted picture. There are as many characterizations of God's anger as there are opinions. But, for an accurate picture, we need to let Scripture describe how God deals with those who rebel against Him.

Accurately portraying God's character was one of the key purposes of Christ's ministry. The claims that Jesus made about himself were so profound, it was difficult for people to accept Him. In John 12:44, He said, "'To believe in me, is not to believe in me but in him who sent me; **to see me, is to see him who sent me**. I have come into the world as light, so that no one who has faith in me should remain in darkness.'" Similarly, Jesus explained, "'When you have lifted up the Son of Man you will know that I am what I am. I do nothing on my own authority, but in all I say, I have been taught by my Father. He who sent me is present with me, and has not left me on my own; for I always do what is pleasing to him'" (John 8:28–29). Jesus goes even one step further: "I do not speak on my own authority, but the Father who sent me has **himself commanded me what to say and how to speak**. I know that his commands are eternal life. **What the Father has said to me, therefore—that is what I speak**'" (John 12:49–50). In short, there is no difference between the character of Jesus and of our heavenly Father. Jesus is our perfect visual aid!

It is because we have not grasped the perfect correlation between the characters of our heavenly Father and of Jesus that we continue to struggle with discovering the simple, yet all-encompassing, relevance of God in our lives. When we see His character, we cannot help but stand in awe of His love, compassion, patience, and mercy. This also means we will understand His righteous anger. It will not appear either harsh or arbitrary.

Tragically, we also either fail to acknowledge the existence of Satan, or to understand his power. Peter warns us, "Be on the alert! Wake up! Your enemy the devil, like a roaring lion, prowls around looking for someone to devour" (1 Peter 5:8). To understand the reason for Satan's mood, John writes, "he who day and night accuses them before our God is overthrown.... Therefore rejoice, you heavens and you that dwell in them! But woe to you, earth and sea, for the Devil has come down to you in great fury, knowing that his time is short" (Revelation 12:10, 12).

Satan has learned he's most successful when he distorts God's character, denies Jesus' divinity, and obscures God's purpose. He attempts to pin the responsibility for His destructive acts on God. He orchestrates situations that are designed to bring out the worst in us. He encourages doubt by whispering ideas like these:

➤ Faith must be practical—God doesn't really stand by the promises in His word.
➤ If God is so loving, why does He allow all this to happen?
➤ You have no potential; your dreams are not achievable.
➤ You're not good enough to be accepted by God or by others.
➤ You're all alone; if you're going get what you deserve, you'd best take things into your own hands
➤ Your achievements are not blessings from God; you did it yourself.

The last thing Satan wants is for us to experience God's power in our lives. He knows that once we've "tasted and seen that the LORD is good" (Psalm 34:8) we'll crave Him, causing Satan to lose his hold on us and on those who witness the great things God does in our lives. Satan uses the horrible acts we witness to encourage us to question whether we serve an all powerful, loving God.

Like any father, God does get angry. His reasons for getting angry are familiar to loving, responsible parents who want the best for their children. So, let's look at what makes parents angry.

1. When someone mistreats their kids.
2. When their children mistreat others or knowingly behave inappropriately.
3. When their child's deliberate actions distort people's view of them as parents.

4. When, despite repeated counsel, their children persist in behaving in a way that will bring them pain.

Because He loves us, God wants us to understand both the painful, long-lasting results of sin and His plan for protecting, healing, and delivering us from sin. He wants us to understand the cause, effects, and solution for sin. God strives to help us understand the whole picture.

Until this process is complete, He does not display wrath. It's after we have a clear knowledge of what He desires to do in our lives, and we still ignore Him, that we witness His anger. Let's turn to a couple of examples in Scripture.

The disciples asked if a man was born blind because of his own sins or his parents' sins. Jesus answered, "'He was born blind so that God's power might be displayed in curing him. While daylight lasts we must carry on the work of him who sent me; night is coming, when no one can work'" (John 9:3–4).

Jesus' answer was, No, the man wasn't born blind because of his or his parents' sins. Jesus' intention was to demonstrate God's love, power, and individual concern for the man. He sets the record straight when he says, "'It is for judgment that I have come into this world—to give sight to the sightless and to make blind those who see'" (v. 39).

This man, who was born physically blind, was also blind to our heavenly Father's true nature. Meanwhile, those who claimed to know our God were the ones who were truly blind. Conclusion: instead of anger, God has nothing but compassion toward those who have not been given the opportunity to know His true nature.

Similarly, in the book of Luke, Jesus refers to two terrible situations:

> At that time some people came and told him about the Galileans whose blood Pilate had mixed with their sacrifices. He answered them: 'Do you suppose that, because these Galileans suffered this fate, they must have been greater sinners than anyone else in Galilee?'... Or the eighteen people who were killed when the tower fell on them at Siloam—do you imagine they must have been more guilty than all the other people living in Jerusalem? No, I tell you.' (Luke 13:1–2, 4–5).

Jesus clearly states that these individuals were not greater sinners. However, he also says that, unless the people asking the question repent, they would all meet the same end. Those asking the question clearly believed that they were in better shape than those who were not Jews, but that's not how Jesus saw it! Bad things happen, but it's not necessarily because of God's anger.

In the story of Jonah, he fled because he knew that God was loving and patient. He knew that if he went to Nineveh, the people might actually turn their lives around and God wouldn't punish them. As a result, Jonah felt that he would look foolish. When this actually happened, Jonah was angry with God. As a part of his prayer, he said, "I knew that you are a gracious and compassionate God, long-suffering, ever constant, always ready to relent and not inflict punishment." God then asks Jonah, "'Are you right to be angry?'" (Jonah 4:2, 4). What a fascinating twist!

God demonstrates his amazing love, patience, compassion, mercy, and forgiveness in the final verse when he explains, "And should not I be sorry about the great city of Nineveh, with its hundred and twenty thousand people who cannot tell their right hand from their left, as well as cattle without number?" (Jonah 4:11).

We see the same patience when Abraham pleads with God to save Sodom and Gomorrah. Certainly Abraham knew of the immorality that existed there; however, he receives God's assurance that if there are even fifty moral people, the city will be spared. There is no sign of impatience from God as Abraham continues to bargain. When he's finished, the Lord has agreed to save the city if there are just ten good people. This is hardly the picture of a hotheaded God eager to inflict punishment. "'Have I any desire for the death of a wicked person? says the Lord God. Is not my desire rather that he should mend his ways and live?'" (Ezekiel 18:23).

We've seen that God is no respecter of persons. Moses stressed this to Israel, saying,

> When the Lord your God drives them out before you, do not say to yourselves, 'It is because of our merits that the Lord has brought us in to occupy this land.' It is not because of your merit or your integrity that you are entering their land to occupy it; it is because of the

wickedness of these nations that the LORD your God is
driving them out before you. (Deuteronomy 9:4–5)

Moses also warned them, "Do not give the land a reason to vomit
you out for defiling it, as it will vomit out the people who live there
now" (Leviticus 18:28 NLT).

God wants us to enjoy the blessing of intimacy—first, intimacy
with God, then with our spouses, and finally within the community
of believers. This is why He warns Israel about following the immoral
practices of the heathen nations. Scripture records repeated instances
of sexual immorality and dishonesty, both within Israel and among the
surrounding nations.

Remember, the Israelites had been slaves in a country immersed
in immoral and dysfunctional practices for 400 years. Picture the most
lawless, immoral community you can think of. Then ask yourself
what it would take for God to establish a functional society in that
community. What would they need to take God seriously?

If God was going to be successful with Israel, He would have to
mix love and patience with warnings and punishment. Consequently,
each of the following problems was punishable by death:

➢ A prophet that preaches rebellion by encouraging people to
  disregard God's commandments (Deuteronomy 13:1–5)
➢ Individuals choosing to serve other gods (Deuteronomy
  17:1–7)
➢ Individuals falsely accusing others of committing crimes
  (Deuteronomy 19:16–21)
➢ Sexual immorality, including adultery (Deuteronomy
  22:21–23)

For each of these offences, Moses uses the phrase, "You must rid
yourselves of this wickedness." God had to solve these problems quickly,
once and for all.

I learned from my father that if you want to eliminate a problem,
you need to stop talking about the problem. Instead, counsel, warn, and,
if the offense is repeated, punish. This deterrent prevents reoccurrences.
Once the lesson is learned, the problem virtually goes away. Here's an
example that will make you chuckle.

My parents didn't tolerate the wasting of food. When we were
young children, they acted swiftly to teach us this lesson. One Sabbath

morning when I was five years old, I was taking too long to eat my Cream of Wheat. Dad warned that if I didn't finish, I'd have to eat it later. Well, that didn't get my attention. So, when it was time to leave for church, the cereal was put in the refrigerator.

After church, a couple of families came over for lunch. As I walked into my home, I could smell the food being warmed up. As you might imagine, I was really hungry. When I entered the kitchen, my father reminded me that before I could enjoy Mom's cooking, I had to finish my breakfast. But when Cream of Wheat cools, it's one solid lump. It's awful! No matter how you try to smash the lumps, you won't get the original smooth consistency. I pled with my father to let me eat it on Sunday morning. I got a firm "no"! Once the cereal was warmed, I quickly ate it, lumps and all, and finished just as our friends arrived.

This was the first and last time this happened. My parents effectively taught me the lesson. As you might guess, they have forgotten the incident.

Now let's fast-forward forty-seven years. I had the same problem with my children. A couple of months ago, my daughter was home from college. She was telling my wife and I about a conversation she had with a friend regarding family discipline. She reminded us that I had made her re-warm her hot cereal and eat it before she could have her lunch. She told her friend this only happened once and she had effectively learned the lesson that food was not to be wasted. Just like my father, I had totally forgotten about the incident. Why? Because it had only happened once. I never had to repeat the punishment.

This is what God was trying to do with Israel. His hope was that they would believe Him and that He would never have to administer the punishment. However, if He did, He hoped it would happen just once. The punishment was designed to effectively eliminate these offences from the community if a simple warning wasn't enough.

In *The Tipping Point*, Malcom Gladwell describes the secret to dramatically reducing New York City's rampant crime. He describes the principle of "The Broken Window." In short, city officials learned that when small crimes are overlooked, it emboldens people to pursue more grievous crimes. City officials were shocked to learn that when they cleaned up the graffiti on New York City subways, the murder rate also fell.

God understood this principle. What may appear to be a rather harsh sentence was actually given as a deterrent to create and maintain a cohesive and harmonious society.

As I mentioned earlier, in keeping with God's character of fairness, Israel was warned not to engage in adultery, homosexuality, incest, or sexual intercourse with animals. Paul also describes the problem that God was trying to eliminate:

> Their minds are closed, they are alienated from the life that is in God, because ignorance prevails among them and their hearts have grown hard as stone. Dead to all feeling, they have abandoned themselves to vice, and there is no indecency that they do not practise. (Ephesians 4:18–19)

Satan encourages men and women to completely destroy God's gift of intimacy within a community. He knows that infidelity and promiscuity create scars of distrust, which discourage us from trusting God. The impact is especially hard on children. How are they to learn behaviors that encourage intimacy? How are they to learn to trust people or God? While anything is possible, their parents have created a steep learning curve. Consequently, God's anger is roused. It's important to note that God places adultery and homosexuality on the same level. The punishment for both was the same: death. We've already seen that the disregard for the poor is closely tied to the occurrence of sexual immorality in a community.

God gave Israel an evangelistic mission: to demonstrate God's relevance to the world. He wanted the world to know that the solution to their problems was the example set by Israel. Instead, they did as we have done; they took a beautiful message and ritualized it. In the process, the beauty was lost, the relevance was never realized, and those whom God had intended to touch were left suffering their self-inflicted pain. Stephen's scathing indictment sums it up well: "'How stubborn you are, heathen still at heart and deaf to the truth! You always resist the Holy Spirit. You are just like your fathers!...You received the law given by God's angels and yet you have not kept it'" (Acts 7:51, 53).

A review of Israel's history once again demonstrates God's generosity, patience, mercy, compassion, and, finally, his anger. In the end, it didn't matter what God did to demonstrate His love and power. Israel consistently showed a lack of faith and courage to take Him at his word. Repeatedly, we see the Lord telling Moses, "How much longer will they refuse to trust me in spite of all the signs I have shown among them?" God is so frustrated, He threatens to strike them with pestilence, deny them their heritage, and make Moses' descendants into a greater nation. (Numbers 14:11–12).

What's the lesson we should learn from this? Our absence of faith prevents us from taking the steps to realize the blessings God's promised. Instead, we insist on taking the seemingly practical, common sense approach. This is disobedience. We just can't believe God will really to do for us what He says. We have difficulty believing that He'll act at all!

In Zephaniah, the Lord summarized a recurring situation in which he punished those "who turned their backs on the LORD, who have neither sought the LORD nor consulted him" (Zephaniah 1:6). He promises, "I will search with lanterns in Jerusalem's darkest corners to find and punish those who **sit contented in their sins**, indifferent to the LORD, **thinking he will do nothing at all to them**" (Zephaniah 1:12 NLT, emphasis supplied). God is angry with those who know better! He punishes them because He's run out of options. He wants them to wake up. The all-powerful Creator doesn't know what else to do.

> "See, I will melt them in a crucible and test them like metal. What else can I do with them? For their tongues aim lies like poisoned arrows. They promise peace to their neighbors while planning to kill them. Should I not punish them for this?" asks the LORD. "Should I not avenge myself against a nation such as this?" (Jeremiah 9:7–9 NLT).

God also expresses His profound sense of grief:

> There is no cure for my grief; I am sick at heart....I am wounded by my people's wound; I go about in mourning, overcome with horror. Is there no balm in Gilead, no physician there? Why has no new skin grown over their wound? Would that my head were a spring of water, my eyes a fountain of tears, that I might weep day and night for the slain of my people. Would that I had in the

wilderness a wayside shelter, that I might leave my people
and go away! (Jeremiah 8:18, 21–9:2)

God summarizes the offenses He sees in Israel. He describes them as
foolish and senseless people with eyes that see nothing and ears that hear
nothing. In spite of knowing God's power, they have no fear of God.
He goes on to call many of them scoundrels who "prey on their fellows.
Their houses are full of fraud, as a cage is full of birds. They grow great
and rich, sleek and bloated; they turn a blind eye to wickedness and
refuse to do justice; the claims of the fatherless they do not uphold, nor
do they defend the poor at law" (Jeremiah 5:26–28).

They've mistaken His patience for unwillingness to act. He describes
them as rebellious and defiant, placing full responsibility on these foolish
people for the changes in nature. He tells Jeremiah,

> They did not say to themselves, 'Let us fear the LORD our
> God, who gives the rains of autumn and spring showers
> in their turn, who brings us unfailingly fixed harvest
> seasons.' But *your wrongdoing has upset nature's order, and
> your sins have kept away her bounty.* (Jeremiah 5:24–25,
> emphasis supplied)

How many churches leaders refuse to confront blatant problems
among their members? How many times have you heard them say, "We
mustn't be judgmental," or "We just need to love the person"? In Acts 5,
look at how quickly and directly Peter dealt with Ananias and Sapphira
when they lied to create a façade of generosity. Peter identified the sin
and God's Holy Spirit dealt out the punishment. Ananias and Sapphira
deceived themselves, believing that as long as they donated something
to the church, they were free to create a false impression.

The key point here is that God's anger was seen within His
community of believers. In short, when "the name of God is profaned
among the Gentiles," God is angered (Romans 2:24). Why? Because,
as we learned earlier, it is through us that God's power is seen, His
relevance determined, and His promises fulfilled. When we take on
His name and act contrary to His character, we deprive people of
experiencing the joy, deliverance, and transformation He longs to give.
We are hurting His children, both within the community of believers
and those outside! He doesn't take this lightly.

There are no other instances of such immediate displays of God's anger in the New Testament. It's also important to note that Peter's role in this case was simply to reveal their sin. He didn't decide on the punishment.

Throughout the Bible, God's pattern is to exercise considerable patience before displaying His anger. In fact, His patience is so great that people misinterpret it to mean that He either doesn't care or will do nothing. God understands that Satan has so distorted our image of Him that we can't see who He really is. Therefore, because of His great love, He goes to great lengths to show us His true character.

Ezekiel 20 recounts God's tremendous patience. There are four recurring themes seen throughout the Old Testament that are summarized in this chapter. First, God's promise to give Israel the best land. Second, the laws God gave were for *their benefit* that they might enjoy life. Third, although Israel repeatedly refused to follow the Lord, God kept His promise for the honor of His name. Lastly, He allowed them to experience the full impact of their dysfunctional choices. This also meant He would not participate in their charade; He wouldn't listen to their insincere show of consulting Him when they had no desire to follow His counsel.

Just before Moses' death, the Lord revealed to him some of Israel's future unwise choices. God provided Israel with both warnings and words of encouragement for them to remember as they approached these crossroads. Moses tells them that, if anyone should flatter himself by believing he can ignore God's counsel and still reap His blessings,

> This will bring sweeping disaster. The LORD will not be willing to forgive him; but his anger and resentment will overwhelm this person, and the curses described in this book will fall heavily on him....Your children who follow you and the foreigners who come from distant countries, will see the plagues of the land, the diseases that the LORD has brought upon its people, the whole land burnt up with brimstone and salt, nothing sown, nothing growing....Then they...will ask, 'Why has the LORD so afflicted this land? Why this great outburst of anger?' The answer will be: 'Because they forsook the covenant of the LORD the God of their forefathers. (Deuteronomy 29:19–20, 22–25).

Here, God used Moses to appeal to those suffering the effects of disregarding His counsel. Scripture tells us that God often uses people who *do* understand His character to plead with those going astray. David, Solomon, Jeremiah, Isaiah, Ezekiel, and Daniel all served in this capacity. They also pled to the Lord on Israel's behalf.

As we saw earlier, God also uses events to get our attention. Moses writes,

> If after all this you will not listen to me, I shall go on to punish you seven times over for your sins. I shall break down your stubborn pride. I shall make the sky above you like iron, the earth beneath you like bronze. Your strength will be spent in vain; your land will not yield its produce, nor the trees in it their fruit. If you still defy me and refuse to listen, I shall increase your calamities seven times, as your sins deserve. (Leviticus 26:18–21)

Years later, through Jeremiah, God again reminds Israel what the results of their stubbornness will be.

> Like an Arab lurking in the desert you sat by the wayside to catch lovers; you defiled the land with your adultery and debauchery. Therefore the showers were withheld and the spring rain failed. But yours was a prostitute's brazenness, and you were resolved to show no shame. (Jeremiah 3:2–3)

> People may swear by the life of the LORD, but in fact they perjure themselves. LORD, are your eyes not set upon the truth? You punished them, but they took no heed; you pierced them to the heart, but they refused to learn. They made their faces harder than flint; they refused to repent. I said, 'After all, these are the poor, these are folk without understanding, who do not know the way of the LORD, the ordinances of their God. I shall go to the great ones and speak with them; for they will know the way of the LORD, the ordinances of their God.' But they too have broken the yoke and snapped their traces. (Jeremiah 5:2–5)

But with the punishment, a promise is also given:

> If you and your children turn back to him and obey him
> heart and soul in all that I command you this day, then the
> LORD your God will restore your fortunes....The LORD
> your God will circumcise your hearts and the hearts of
> your descendants, so that you will love him with all your
> heart and soul and you will live....The LORD your God
> will make you more than prosperous in all that you do,
> in the fruit of your body and of your cattle and in the
> fruits of your soil; for, when you obey the LORD your God
> by keeping his commandments and statutes, as they are
> written in this book of the law, and when your turn back
> to the LORD your God with all your heart and soul, he will
> again rejoice over you and be good to you, as he rejoiced
> over your forefathers. (Deuteronomy 30:2–3, 6, 9–10)

Despite our ongoing ignorance and disobedience, God gives some
of the most beautiful promises as a part of our restoration. The promise
given by Moses is repeated years later by Jeremiah:

> For this is the covenant I shall establish with the Israelites
> after those days, says the LORD: I shall set my law within
> them, writing it on their hearts; I shall be their God, and
> they will be my people. No longer need they teach one
> another, neighbour or brother, to know the LORD; all of
> them, high and low alike, will know me, says the LORD,
> for I shall forgive their wrong doing, and their sin I shall
> call to mind no more. (Jeremiah 31:33–34)

Christ clearly identifies the role of those who have taken His name.

> 'You are light for all the world. A town that stands on a hill
> cannot be hidden. When a lamp is lit, it is not put under
> the meal-tub, but on the lamp stand, where it gives light
> to everyone in the house. Like the lamp, you must shed
> light among your fellows, so that, **when they see the
> good you do, they may give praise to your Father
> in heaven**.' (Matthew 5:14–16, emphasis supplied)

155

We're called to make the world a better place. By our example, people will hear God's call, collectively show sin's terrible blight, and experience the peace and joy that God intended.

As increasing numbers of people ignore God's counsel, the painful effects of disobedience will increase. The fewer the number of people who pray for God's intervention and protection, the greater freedom Satan has in spreading destruction. Isaiah describes sin's effects on the earth:

> The earth dries up and withers, the whole world wilts and withers, the heights of the earth wilt. The earth itself is desecrated by those who live on it, for they have broken laws, disobeyed statutes, and violated the everlasting covenant. That is why a curse consumes the earth and its inhabitants suffer punishment, why the inhabitants of the earth dwindle and only a few are left. (Isaiah 24:4–6).

As with any loving parent, God's anger and His discipline are for a purpose: to call us to a life of relevance and transformation, enabling us to spontaneously reach out to share the goodness of our heavenly Father. His anger is a call of restoration. Isaiah 54:5-7, 10 states,

> Your husband is your Maker; his name is the LORD of Hosts. He who is called God of all the earth, the Holy One of Israel, is your redeemer. The LORD has acknowledged you a wife again, once deserted and heart-broken; your God regards you as a wife still young, though you were once cast off. For a passing moment I forsook you, but with tender affection I shall bring you home again.... Though the mountains may move and the hills shake, my love will be immovable and never fail, and my covenant promising peace will not be shaken, says the LORD in his pity for you.

After trying in every way possible to touch the lives of His children, God knows when nothing more can be done. The effects of sin bring increasing pain and suffering on all, God included. It is then that He will act. This brings Him no joy. "As I live, says the Lord GOD, I have no desire for the death of the wicked. I would rather that the wicked should mend their ways and live" (Ezekiel 33:11).

Despite God's many pleas to Israel, they ignored Him. Israel's final chapter is tragic:

> They made their sons and daughters pass through the fire. They practiced augury and divination; they sold themselves to do what was wrong in the eyes of the LORD and so provoked his anger. Thus it was that the LORD was incensed against Israel and banished them from his presence. (2 Kings 17:17–18)

The king of Assyria besieged Israel, captured their king, and deported the people. Israel had become so debased that they forgot how to worship God. Consequently, the king of Assyria ordered that one of captive priests was to teach the people how to worship the God of their country. What a tragic outcome—and totally contrary to God's will. How ironic that instead of God's chosen people teaching the foreigner, the foreigner was teaching them!

The pain inflicted upon others ultimately returns to the individual. Isaiah warns, "Woe betide you, destroyer, yourself undestroyed, betrayer still un-betrayed! After all your destroying, you will be destroyed; after all your betrayals, you yourself will be betrayed" (Isaiah 33:1).

Many, like Jonah, feel God is too patient and merciful. Some even say that, because of His great patience, the righteous end up receiving no benefit as compared to the stubborn. God responds to this opinion through Malachi:

> You have used hard words about me, says the LORD. Yet you ask, 'How have we spoken against you?' You have said, 'to serve God is futile. What do we gain from the LORD of Hosts by observing his rules and behaving with humble submission?' ... They will be mine, says the LORD of Hosts, my own possession against the day that I appoint, and I shall spare them as a man spares the son who serves him. Once more you will tell the good from the wicked, the servant of God from the person who does not serve him. The day comes, burning like a furnace; all the arrogant and all evildoers will be stubble, and that day when it comes will set them ablaze, leaving them neither root nor branch, says the LORD of Hosts. But for you who

fear my name, the sun of righteousness will rise with healing in its wings, and you will break loose like calves released from the stall. On the day I take action, you will tread down the wicked, for they will be as ashes under the soles of your feet, says the LORD of Hosts. (Malachi 3:13–14, 17–4:3)

This is an awesome way of life to embrace—and to share! God sent His son to make the beauty of the eternal gospel burn brighter to attract us and motivate us to begin a life of transformation and renewal. Will we accept and embrace the purpose of God's anger and return to Him by loving Him with all our hearts? Will we step out in faith, allowing Him, through the grace of Jesus, to work powerfully in our lives to touch those around us?

It is by keeping God's commands that we can be sure we know him. Whoever says, 'I know him,' but does not obey his commands, is a liar and the truth is not in him; but **whoever is obedient to his word, in him the love of God is truly made perfect**. This is how we can be sure that we are in him: whoever claims to be dwelling in him **must live as Christ himself lived**. (1 John 2:3–6, emphasis supplied)

That out of the treasures of his glory he may grant you inward strength and power through his Spirit, that through faith Christ may dwell in your hearts in love. With deep roots and firm foundations may you, in company with all God's people, be strong to grasp what is the breadth and length and height and depth of Christ's love, and to know it, though it is beyond knowledge. **So may you be filled with the very fullness of God**. (Ephesians 3:16–19, emphasis supplied)

Action Steps

1. How have the scriptures in this chapter changed your view of God? Does this view give you a stronger desire to draw closer to God?

2. How does this view increase your compassion for those who don't know God?

3. Does this view create a greater desire to follow God's counsel and not take Him for granted? Why?

4. Think of someone who will be blessed by what you've learned. Ask God for an opportunity to share your newfound joy.

Additional Scripture for Study

1. Psalm 29:5
2. Isaiah 42:18–43:2
3. Hebrews 10:26–31; 12:18–29
4. 2 Peter 3:9–15
5. Jude 1
6. Revelation 20:4–15; 21:1–7

Chapter 10

Spontaneous Sharing

Hidden

Gem:

In the great assembly I have proclaimed what is right; I do not hold back my words, as you know, LORD. I have not kept your goodness hidden in my heart; I have proclaimed your faithfulness and saving power, and have not concealed your unfailing love and truth from the great assembly. (Psalm 40:9–10)

A month ago, some friends invited me to drop by and show them the presentation that I'd prepared for executives of financial institutions. As the last minute preparations for dinner were completed, their son, who's attending college, joined us. He asked me how God fits into the picture when planning our future. I immediately shared my personal story and belief that God both respects and inspires our dreams. I shared a couple of examples from Scripture and challenged him to read the book of Deuteronomy.

The next week at church, he was excited. As I approached him, he was sharing with his friends what he'd found in Deuteronomy. Christianity had a new relevance that he'd never seen before. I had shared my excitement with him and it had become contagious! He was wondering why he'd never heard preached what he had discovered in Deuteronomy.

'As for me, God forbid that I should sin against the Lord by ceasing to pray for you. I shall show you what is right and good: to revere the Lord and worship him faithfully with all our heart; for consider what great things he has done for you. But if you persist in wickedness, both you and your king will be swept away.' (1 Samuel 12:23–25)

Isn't Samuel's choice of words interesting? Israel had just rejected both his and God's leadership, and Samuel prayed, "God forbid that I should sin against the Lord by ceasing to pray for you." Samuel could have said, "They've made their choice; now go live with it!" But God had transformed him. Despite Israel's actions, Samuel still desired only the best for them, displaying God's love and mercy. Samuel prayed, which was his only viable constructive alternative. Not only was his reaction spontaneous, he also accepted his role to help Israel remember the marvelous acts that God had done.

Samuel's spontaneous response is consistent with what we've discovered elsewhere in Scripture. Here's a summary of what we've learned:

1. **All of God's counsel was given to bless us and protect us**. This includes the Law He gave to Moses at Mt. Sinai.

2. **A supportive and functional community results from obeying God's law.** While God's law was given to bless us, it was only meant as the starting point. When we joyfully make it the center point of our lives and our community, God is vindicated.

3. **God can be trusted**. His promises never fail, and they are for all of us. He is no respecter of persons. He has no favorites. This means that each of us has direct access to Him. We don't need a go-between since Jesus, our brother and Savior, is at the right hand of God. This also means that there is no downside risk. We're not giving up a thing. His promises are given to provide guidance, hope, deliverance, and healing—now! All the ways of the Lord are loving and sure. God only acts in our best interest!

4. **Through the death and resurrection of Jesus Christ, God desires to restore us to His image and**

transform our lives into something beyond our wildest imaginations.

5. **We come to desire His guidance in our lives,** understanding that sin is anything that keeps us from the blessings God wants to give us. We want to find the sin in our lives, since it prevents us from fully experiencing these blessings.

6. **God is very slow to anger,** even though He is all-powerful. He understands how much Satan has distorted His character. He also understands how ignorant we are about His character and about the wonderful things He wants to do in our lives. When God displays anger, it is either to wake us up, or to punish those whose hardened hearts makes their influence so damaging that He must step in.

7. **The only way that God's character can be vindicated is by our personal experience.** He is anxious for us to experience His purpose for our lives. He wants us to take Him at His word and make His promises a reality. When we do, He'll create such an awesome experience that *we will spontaneously share our story with those around us.* This will encourage them also to "taste and see that the Lord is good".

8. **Satan does not want us to experience God's goodness.** You've heard of the saying, "Misery loves company." Well, that's Satan's situation. He knows what he's given up, and he doesn't want us to figure it out! Consequently, he does all he can to distort God's character, fill us with fear and doubt, and destroy us outright.

Besides the desire to share his own firsthand experiences, why did Samuel feel such an obligation to continue praying for Israel? He loved them and saw their potential. But, he was painfully watching the prophecies God gave Moses come true. He saw that the situation would get worse if they continued this course of action. Only prayer could reverse their slide.

When I've shared my excitement with what God has done in my life, I've never had anyone stop me and say, "I don't want to hear this!"

Instead, they express surprise, and they wonder if God would do the same in their own lives. It gives me such a thrill to say that I absolutely know He will. He's just waiting for them to give Him the chance. When they leave, they are filled with a sense of wonder and curiosity. In the Gospels, when Christ touched someone's life, people's response was predictable: "They were all lost in amazement and praised God; filled with awe they said, 'The things we have seen today are beyond belief!'" (Luke 5:26).

Satan has effectively kept us from realizing that God wants to do something special in our lives. Satan is not idly sitting around, waiting for someone to experience God's power in his life. Not a chance! He understands the necessity of taking preventive action. The last thing he wants is to have another person passing on the excitement of the new truth they've found. You can bet that he's going to double his efforts to distract us, distort the truth, and confuse the situation.

This is why a key part of a powerful prayer life includes claiming the promises God has given us. Isaiah foretold the impact that God's people would have when they systematically claimed God's promises and shared the eternal gospel.

> The spirit of the Lord GOD is upon me because the LORD has anointed me; he has sent me to announce good news to the humble, to bind up the broken-hearted, to proclaim liberty to captives, release to those in prison...to give them garlands instead of ashes, oil of gladness instead of mourners' tears, a garment of splendour for the heavy heart. (Isaiah 61:1, 3)

Stop and consider the difference we each can make when we share what God is doing in our lives. Sharing starts within our family, within our church, and with those we meet daily. When we share, it's not work. No classes are needed. There's no special technique. When we're excited, it just flows! Our friends and family know when we're excited. They know it's real.

Let's say that, each day, I share with just two people the wonderful things God is doing in my life. This means that, during the month, I would have shared God's goodness with 60 people. Of these sixty people, let's say that just one of them (1.7 percent) catches my enthusiasm and they share with two people each day. A seemingly miniscule 1.7 percent of the total gets excited about what the Lord has done in their lives. Let's say this sequence is repeated over the next thirty-six months. At the end of thirty-seven months, 8.25 billion lives will have been touched, and there will be a total of 137.4 million excited people. As of today, February 12, 2010, at 7:17 p.m. EST, the world population is 6.8 billion, which means we would have surpassed the world's population. We could cover a lot of ground in just three years!

Connecting with two people every day may seem aggressive, so you choose the time period that seems reasonable to you. For example, if I share with five people every month, I will reach 60 people in a year. At that rate, the good news will reach everyone in 36 years. If I share with 10 people each month, the entire world's population would have come in contact with someone who's been awed by what God's done in their lives in just 18 years. This assumes that you're the only person in the world who loves Jesus. It seems almost too simple to believe that there could be such a big impact so quickly. But here are the numbers:

Time Period	People with Gratitude	People who Caught Fire	Total People with Gratitude	People whose Lives were Touched
1	1	1	2	60
2	2	2	4	180
3	4	4	8	420
4	8	8	16	900
5	16	16	32	1,860
6	32	32	64	3,780
7	64	64	128	7,620
8	128	128	256	15,300
9	256	256	512	30,660
10	512	512	1,024	61,380
11	1,024	1,024	2,048	122,820
12	2,048	2,048	4,096	245,700
13	4,096	4,096	8,192	491,460
14	8,192	8,192	16,384	982,980
15	16,384	16,384	32,768	1,966,020
16	32,768	32,768	65,536	3,932,100
17	65,536	65,536	131,072	7,864,260
18	131,072	131,072	262,144	15,728,580

19	262,144	262,144	524,288	31,457,220
20	524,288	524,288	1,048,576	62,914,500
21	1,048,576	1,048,576	2,097,152	125,829,060
22	2,097,152	2,097,152	4,194,304	251,658,180
23	4,194,304	4,194,304	8,388,608	503,316,420
24	8,388,608	8,388,608	16,777,216	1,006,632,900
25	16,777,216	16,777,216	33,554,432	2,013,265,860
26	33,554,432	33,554,432	67,108,864	4,026,531,780
27	67,108,864	67,108,864	134,217,728	8,053,063,620
28	134,217,728	134,217,728	268,435,456	16,106,127,300
29	268,435,456	268,435,456	536,870,912	32,212,254,660
30	536,870,912	536,870,912	1,073,741,824	64,424,509,380
31	1,073,741,824	1,073,741,824	2,147,483,648	128,849,018,820
32	2,147,483,648	2,147,483,648	4,294,967,296	257,698,037,700
33	4,294,967,296	4,294,967,296	8,589,934,592	515,396,075,460
34	8,589,934,592	8,589,934,592	17,179,869,184	1,030,792,150,980
35	17,179,869,184	17,179,869,184	34,359,738,368	2,061,584,302,020
36	34,359,738,368	34,359,738,368	68,719,476,736	4,123,168,604,100
37	68,719,476,736	68,719,476,736	137,438,953,472	8,246,337,208,260

If you're asking why this hasn't happened before, it has! Look at the exponential growth that occurred in the early Christian church. They were excited—thrilled—with what the Lord had done for them. It has even happened during our lives—though, unfortunately, not in the church. In Malcolm Gladwell's book, *Tipping Point*, he identifies trends, both good and bad, that have spread like a pandemic virus. One fad in particular caught my attention: the rebirth of the Hush Puppy shoe. In 1994, annual sales of Hush Puppy shoes had fallen to just 30,000—so low that they were making plans to discontinue the shoe. But because of some kids in Manhattan who ran into a couple of designers, sales skyrocketed. By 1995, 430,000 pairs were sold and, in 1996, 1.7 million were sold!

Gladwell identifies the characteristics necessary for a social epidemic. Interestingly, these are characteristics shared in a community of believers that has been profoundly touched by God. Here are a few of the elements:

1. A small percentage of people do most of the work. We just demonstrated this characteristic.

2. The people involved have a passion for being *connected to people*. They are profusely positive and full of energy. Some have the gift of bringing people together, others accumulate information, and others have the gift of persuasion. Usually, these are not characteristics a person can develop, but I've witnessed naturally shy people develop an infectious enthusiasm that enables them to be effective public speakers.
3. The idea must have what Gladwell calls "stickiness." It must be *both* memorable and rouse people to action.

This reminds me of the story of the demon-possessed man that Christ healed.

> Eyewitnesses told them how the madman had been cured. Then **the whole population of the Gerasene district was overcome by fear** and asked Jesus to go away. So he got into the boat and went away. The man from whom the demons had gone out begged to go with him; but Jesus sent him away: 'Go back home,' he said, 'and tell them what God has done for you.' The man went all over the town proclaiming what Jesus had done for him. (Luke 8:36–39, emphasis supplied)

It does not appear that there were many eye witnesses; however, the word flew through the district quickly and the people asked Jesus to leave. Consider the reaction of each person who heard what had happened. **They felt personally affected; it was urgent that the word got out**. Each person quickly told someone else. In a matter of a few hours the whole district was overcome by fear.

Let's say that two witnesses ran back to town and each told just one other person about what Jesus did. If this sequence were repeated only nineteen times, a total of 1,048,576 people would have heard! Just ten times, and a total of 2,048 people would have heard. These people were energized by the fear of economic loss after losing a large herd of pigs. The message they communicated was that Jesus was bad news! These witnesses had credibility; consequently, their message of alarm spread like wildfire!

But certainly each person would have told more than one person.

So, let's assume that each person tells three people. Now the message needs to be passed on just 12 times to reach 1,048,576 people. To spread the news to 2,048 people it would take just a bit over six times. Now we can see how it took so little time for the people of the district to ask Jesus to leave.

The good news is that when Jesus returned later, crowds of people welcomed him. The process had been reversed, and, once again, it began with just one man—the man who was healed—giving witness about what Jesus had done for him.

What about our friend the demoniac? He was well-known, but for all the wrong reasons. The community was afraid of him; they had unsuccessfully tried to ensure their safety by keeping him in chains. After Jesus left and the ex-demoniac entered town, people were undoubtedly guarded, waiting for another "outburst." They probably even felt sorry for his relatives. Think of the family who had suffered years of embarrassment and guilt, wishing that this problem would go away. Suddenly, the source of their angst is back in their home.

The demoniac started a new epidemic, beginning with his family. They could now say with certainty that he was no longer a threat to the community. His talents were restored, and he began a new life as a productive member of society. His message was clear, simple, and filled with gratitude: "I've been healed and Jesus can heal you too!" His message was so effective that when Jesus returned, a dramatically different pictured is described. Crowds came to see Him. About 4,000 people stayed with Him for three days.

Everything Jesus did was relevant and personal to people's lives. His message was vibrant. People wanted to hear more. He longed to help the people who came to Him. In Mark 8:2, Jesus says, "'My heart goes out to these people; they have been with me now for three days and have nothing to eat.'" Jesus then took seven loaves of bread and three fish and fed them all.

The bottom line? **Small changes bring big results!** The small act of one person telling someone else quickly had a large impact. This is the rule of compounding in action. The power of compounding is stressed in creating financial wealth; however, it's equally applicable in viral epidemics and fads. It happened during the early years of the Protestant Reformation. Learning that salvation was neither earned nor prevented by the church was exciting. It was relevant. People had to share the message.

This is what we need today. And it starts with us. We begin by claiming His promises, joyfully obeying His counsel, and believing He will do as He's promised. We will then "taste and see that the Lord is good."

What is your message? If you were given just two minutes to share with someone, what would you say? Would it move the person to action? Too often we assume that someone's lack of interest is because they've rejected God. This attitude is wrong. Many people have correctly rejected the distorted vision of God by observing "Christian" actions. Their heart will be stirred when they witness Jesus dwelling and working in the life of someone they know.

> As witnesses for Christ, **we are to tell what we know, what we ourselves have seen and heard and felt**. If we have been following Jesus step by step, **we shall have something right to the point to tell concerning the way in which He has led us.** We can tell how we have tested His promise, and found the promise true. We can bear witness to what we have known of the grace of Christ. This is the witness for which our Lord calls, and for want of which the world is perishing. (*Desire of Ages*, page 340)

David said,

> In the great assembly I have proclaimed what is right; I do not hold back my words, as you know, LORD. I have not kept your goodness hidden in my heart; I have proclaimed your faithfulness and saving power, and have not concealed your unfailing love and truth from the great assembly. You, LORD, will not withhold your tender care from me; may your love and truth forever guard me. (Psalm 40:9–11)

The Holy Spirit always has the same effect on those whose hearts are open to receiving a glimpse of God's goodness. We see it in the book of Psalms and throughout the gospels. We're not to be spectators but participants in spreading this good news. Paul reminds us in Ephesians 5:1, "In a word, as God's dear children you must be like him." The mission that our Father in heaven gave Jesus is our mission too. Jesus says, "As you sent me into the world, I have sent them into the world, and for their sake I consecrate myself, that they too may be consecrated by the truth" (John 17:19).

In short, God has an exciting message that He wants us to share. It will result in people being awed and praising our heavenly Father. The Holy Spirit will guide us to a fuller knowledge of God and will begin to transform us so that we will glorify God and bring Him the praise due Him.

Satan has always known just how simple it would be to share God's love and spread this excitement. Now you can see why he's so intent on keeping God's image distorted and keeping us distracted. He understands that the combined power of prayer and God's promises far exceeds the power of evil. Too many of us believe that someone else's prayers are more powerful than ours, but that's not true. God's will is that our attitudes change. As we commit ourselves to learning to pray, God is waiting to show His power.

At the very beginning of Israel's journey from Egypt, God gave them a promise: "If only you will now listen to me and keep my covenant, then out of all peoples you will become my special possession; for the whole earth is mine. You will be to me a **kingdom of priests**, my holy nation" (Exodus 19:5–6, emphasis supplied). Note the phrase, "a kingdom of priests." There's no exclusivity. This is certainly a foreign concept for most of us. God has given us an opportunity to partner with Him to make a difference in the lives of those we care about. We each have the privilege of direct and immediate access to our heavenly Father for the benefit of those we present to God. If you believe your pastor, bishop, or priest has access to God that you don't, that's not what God believes. Step out of your comfort zone; claim a promise and watch what happens!

When Israel chose to worship the golden calf, and the Levites challenged Moses and Aaron's authority, God was forced to establish priests who would intercede for people; through them He would communicate His will. This was a result of their disobedience, but God wasn't happy with the arrangement. Neither was Israel. Even then, the people understood the importance of the limitation this arrangement created. "The Israelites said to Moses, 'This is the end of us! We must perish, one and all! Everyone who goes near the Tabernacle of the LORD will die. Is this to be our final end?'" (Numbers 17:12-13).

Of course, we know this wasn't the final outcome, but a temporary measure. God clearly desires to restore direct communication with each of us. He promised Jeremiah,

> For this is the covenant I shall establish with the Israelites after those days, says the LORD: I shall set my law within them, writing it on their hearts; I shall be their God, and they will be my people. **No longer need they teach one another, neighbour or brother, to know the LORD; all of them, high and low alike, will know me, says the LORD, for I shall forgive their wrongdoing, and their sin I shall call to mind no more**. (Jeremiah 31:33–34, emphasis supplied)

This promise was fulfilled through Christ's death and resurrection, which reestablished our direct line of communication.

John encouraged us to approach the Lord confidently with our prayers.

> **We can approach God with this confidence**: if we make requests which accord with his will, he listens to us; and if we know that our requests are heard, we also know that all we ask of him is ours. If anyone sees a fellow-Christian committing a sin which is not a deadly sin, he should intercede for him, and God will grant him life. (1 John 5:14–16, emphasis supplied)

Paul broadened the scope of our prayers when he said, "First of all, then, I urge that **petitions, prayers, intercessions, and thanksgivings be offered for everyone**, for sovereigns and for all in high office so that we may lead a tranquil and quiet life, free to practise our religion with dignity" (1 Timothy 2:1–2, emphasis supplied). Paul also strongly encouraged us to remember that "the kingdom of God is not a matter of words, but of power" (1 Corinthians 4:20).

Scripture relates examples of common people who confessed the sins of Israel even before Christ came. These people asked that God would hear, forgive, and act. Nehemiah, a cupbearer for the king, prayed:

> 'Let your ear be attentive and your eyes open to my humble prayer, which now day and night I make in your presence on behalf of your servants, the people of Israel. I confess the sins which we Israelites have committed against you, and of which my father's house and I are also guilty. We have acted very wrongly towards you and have not observed the commandments, statutes, and rules which you enjoined on your servant Moses....Lord, let your ear be attentive to my humble prayer, and to the prayer of your servants who delight to revere your name. Grant me success this day, and put it into this man's heart to show me kindness.' (Nehemiah 1:6-7, 11)

Following his prayer, Nehemiah approached the king, and God answered his prayer. King Artaxerxes wrote letters granting Nehemiah safe passage; he also ordered that the necessary materials be supplied to rebuild the wall of Jerusalem and the temple.

Daniel is another example. He, too, was distressed by the plight of Israel. He confesses the sins of Israel:

> 'We have sinned, doing what was wrong and wicked; we have rebelled and rejected your commandments and your decrees. We have turned a deaf ear to your servants the prophets, who spoke in your name to our kings and princes, to our forefathers, and to all the people of the land....Lord, hear; Lord, forgive; Lord, listen and act; God, for your own sake do not delay, because your city and your people bear your name.' (Daniel 9:5–6, 19)

This is our privilege, too! God is waiting to answer our requests. For the honor of His name, He wants us to share the relevance that He can bring to people's lives today. He wants to use each of us to demonstrate that He cares.

Satan understands the impact that a few Spirit-filled, excited people will have on those around them. Consequently, you can expect a fight. Don't be surprised! This is why Paul says,

Put on the full armour provided by God, so that you may be able to stand firm against the stratagems of the devil. For **our struggle is not against human foes, but against cosmic powers, against the authorities and potentates of this dark age, against the superhuman forces of evil** in the heavenly realms. (Ephesians 6:11–12, emphasis supplied)

Paul also reminds us to "Constantly ask God's help in prayer, and pray always in the power of the Spirit. To this end keep watch and persevere, **always interceding** for all God's people" (Ephesians 6:18, emphasis supplied).

Paul puts it all in perspective:

With all this in mind, what are we to say? **If God is on our side, who is against us?** He did not spare his own Son, but gave him up for us all; how can he fail to lavish every other gift upon us? ... Throughout it all, overwhelming victory is ours through him who loved us. For I am convinced that there is nothing in death or life, in the realm of spirits or superhuman powers, in the world as it is or the world as it shall be, in the forces of the universe, in heights or depths—**nothing in all creation that can separate us from the love of God in Christ Jesus our Lord**. (Romans 8:31–32, 37–39, emphasis supplied)

Jesus' prayer to our Father was,

I do not pray you to take them out of the world, but to keep them from the evil one. They are strangers in the world, as I am. Consecrate them by the truth; your word is truth. As you sent me into the world, I have sent them into the world. (John 17:15–18)

By exercising faith, by praising God for His goodness, by reaching out and sharing His goodness, and by praying continually, we can look forward to new experiences that will continue to excite us and fill us with awe for our heavenly Father's loving kindness.

The joy of dwelling with Jesus spontaneously creates excitement and the hope of Jesus' Second Coming. We will look forward with tremendous expectation to the day when we can, with inexpressible joy, look into our Savior's face and be free from Satan's assaults. Paul's words of encouragement take on a whole new meaning:

> This we tell you as a word from the Lord: those of us who are still alive when the Lord comes will have no advantage over those who have died; when the command is given, when the archangel's voice is heard, when God's trumpet sounds, then the Lord himself will descend from heaven; first the Christian dead will rise, then we who are still alive shall join them, caught up in clouds to meet the Lord in the air. Thus we shall always be with the Lord. Console one another, then, with these words. (1 Thessalonians 4:15–18)

When that day finally comes, we'll see the results of all our intercessory prayers. We'll hear how our words of encouragement lifted someone's spirits at a critical time in her life. Like a pebble that's dropped in a pond, we'll see the rippling effect that our testimony has had on people we've never met. Words cannot appropriately express the joy we will experience.

Once we've discovered the plan that God designed to protect, restore, and transform us from sin, once we understand His relevance in our lives today and His vision for us in eternity, we will have a renewed urgency to share this good news with those whom we come in contact.

My prayer is that, with these hidden gems, you'll begin your own journey of discovery. My desire and prayer for you is the same as Paul's prayer in Ephesians:

> I pray that your inward eyes may be enlightened, so that you may know what is the hope to which he calls you, how rich and glorious is the share he offers you among his people in their inheritance, and how vast are the resources of his power open to us who have faith. (Ephesians 1:18–19)

Action Steps

1. Continue reading the Psalms; also, read Acts. Notice that each writer is sharing what he has experienced.

2. Following God's counsel creates new, positive ways of sharing. People will be drawn to know your God. Pray for opportunities to give God the credit for what He's doing in your life.

3. Is it difficult to see what God is doing in your life? Write down what you have asked Him to do and how He answers your requests. Also, ask yourself if you've committed to following His counsel.

4. Ask others who you have heard sharing God's goodness how they started their journey. Write down the action steps they followed.

Additional Scripture for Study

1. Psalm 98

2. Mark 12:29–30; 10:15

3. Review the impact that Jesus had in people's lives. Read Luke 4:31–37; 5:21–26; 8:21, 39; 7:11–17; 17:5–10.

Final Note

After three years, I'm finally ready to send *Hidden Gems* to the publishers. You deserve the latest update of my journey.

It's now June, 2011, and I've been unemployed for exactly two years. Although I've spent the last two years working long hours on developing CashMap, the interactive educational financial tool built exclusively for the iPad, I continue to search for the most effective way to create interest in the project.

Few Americans or Canadians know that, by making a few simple changes in the way they manage their cash, they can save thousands of dollars in interest on their loans. The process is simple. Unfortunately, we are so distracted, and we've been burned by so many scams, that people find it hard to believe there is a legitimate and simple cash management strategy that's not been shared by our nation's top financial counselors.

The poor sales to date have definitely been disappointing. While I've considered walking away from the project and looking for a regular job, I can't because I understand the benefits the software can have on people's lives, and I see God's guiding hand.

As my wife and I watched our cash reserves dwindle, I struggled with what I should do next. With two kids attending a private university, we had to make a decision. My battle with fear began again. I began asking myself if I had acted foolishly and irresponsibly. But I made a decision that I would not complain. Instead, I would pray and wait.

Then I received a phone call from a friend asking me to share the status of the project. After I updated him, he blew me away with his next announcement: he, too, was convinced that God was guiding me. Instead of passively investing his dollars in unknown companies via mutual funds, he preferred to be involved in a company like mine that was working to improve people's lives. I was stunned! My friend is not wealthy. I asked if he'd consulted with his wife, and he assured me that he had. He then told me that he'd called, not to ask my opinion, but to inform me that he was making the investment in my company.

God wasn't done surprising me. A year ago, two patent attorneys told me that it was doubtful I would be able to get a patent for CashMap. Filing a patent is expensive—about $10,000 for domestic patents. They advised me to file a provisional patent, which would give me one year to make a decision. I hired one of the attorneys to file our provisional patent.

Approximately two weeks before the application was set to expire, I called our attorney to review my options. He offered to take a look at CashMap and give me his assessment. Upon reviewing the software, he, too, was impressed. He shared that he believes God gives His children creative skills in order to benefit people's lives. Then he completely surprised me. He offered to file both the domestic and international patents for me in return for an equity share in the company. He estimated the total cost would be $12,000. He had already discussed this with his wife, and she had agreed.

Clearly, God had given me his answer.

A team of MBA students from Seattle University studied CashMap. They too were surprised how few people (themselves included) understood the simple financial concept of optimizing your average daily balance. They were also surprised to find I have virtually no competition. They agreed with our pricing strategy and also agreed that I should pursue securing contracts with banks, credit unions, and investment companies. Their fresh perspective helped us in subsequent product enhancement and validated our conclusions regarding the strategies already in place.

I am in the early phases of discussions with two large financial institutions. One of the companies has provided weekly guidance, sharpening the emotional message of the educational presentations I've created. A trainer for this company has provided invaluable insight.

The staff of Lifetime Cable Channel's, "A Balancing Act" has approached me to produce a five-minute information segment about CashMap. The feature will air in September 2011.

All of the professionals—a couple of bankers, a venture capital executive, software executives, mortgage professionals, and consultants—who have reviewed CashMap have been positively impressed with the quality of the product. Do I wish that sales had enabled us to be self-sustaining within the first six months? Of course! But the reality is that God has provided what I've needed when I needed it.

This story is continuing to unfold. We have significant obstacles facing us that will require God's intervention. I don't know what will happen. There are just three things for me to accomplish: do my best; claim God's promises that He'll guide me and provide for me; and praise Him for whatever happens. I know He'll give me new songs to sing and new experiences to share!

> I have not kept your goodness hidden in my heart; I have proclaimed your faithfulness and saving power, and have not concealed your unfailing love and truth from the great assembly. You, LORD, will not withhold your tender care from me; may your love and truth forever guard me. (Psalm 40:10–11)

Deuteronomy Study Guide

Every aspect of your life will be impacted by a clearer view of our heavenly Father's character. It changes what you expect of Him, how you view His counsel, how you make decisions, and how you communicate with people. This study's focus is to provide insight into His character. It is my prayer that you, too, will be blessed as His character is revealed.

I found that the beauty of Deuteronomy is found in seeing it as God's plan for creating a harmonious and functional society. It gives us a glimpse of a God who, despite sin's entrance, was willing to go out of His way to demonstrate that He wasn't content to sit back and just let things happen. He wants us to know by experience that He cares for us and is worthy of our trust.

In short, the theme of Deuteronomy is, "I love you and want to dwell with you. Trust me—I'm faithful. I have a wonderful journey in store for you that will satisfy the longings of your heart. It will be to your benefit." This is the recurring theme of Scripture: discovering His character and learning to trust Him one step at a time.

Read the passages at the beginning of each section first. Don't feel rushed to finish each section in one sitting. It took our study group an entire year to read the book of Deuteronomy! Take your time, and enjoy your discovery. Look up the references, and see how Scripture fits together like a beautiful tapestry.

As you read each verse, ask yourself the following questions:
1. If I were in this situation, how would I feel? Would I do the

same thing? If not, why not? What does this reveal about the depth of my faith?

2. How can this situation apply to my life now?
3. What lesson can I learn?
4. What new insight does this give me into God's character?
5. What impact can this have regarding how I pray and what I expect from God?
6. What impact can this have on my relationship with others? What changes do I need to make?

Challenge yourself! As you identify the changes you'd like to make in your life, share them with someone and ask that person to pray with and for you. Find a promise that is applicable to your situation. Claim it, act with joyful obedience, and step forward in confidence, knowing He is faithful. Share your answers. Learn from each other and grow. God won't let you down!

Once you've completed this study, you will see the themes presented in Deuteronomy are repeated over and over in both the Old and New Testaments. As you read the gospels and Paul's letters, you'll refer to Deuteronomy time and time again.

Have fun, and may God richly bless you. May your study deepen your faith and renew your appreciation of God's relevance in your life today while you look forward with joyous anticipation to the second coming of Jesus.

Section 1: Background

Before we begin studying Deuteronomy, it is helpful to understand its context. The events in this book came at the end of Moses' life, after the forty years of wandering in the wilderness, and before the entrance into the Promised Land.

The covenant God made with Israel was a renewal of the one He made hundreds of years earlier. In this book, Moses summarized Israel's history and repeated the covenant God made with their ancestors.

God's Covenant to Abraham, Isaac, and Jacob

1. Read about the covenant given to Abraham, Isaac, and Jacob in Genesis 15:18–21, Genesis 26:3–4, Genesis 28:13. What did God promise them?

2. Genesis 15:13–16: How long did God predict that Israel would stay in Egypt?

3. Genesis 46:26–27: How large was Jacob's family when they came to Egypt?

4. Exodus 12:41: How long did Israel actually stay in Egypt?

5. Exodus 13:18: What generation left Egypt?

6. Numbers 1:45–46; Exodus 12:37: Estimate how many people left Egypt. (Note: these verses just give an estimate of the men, not including wives, children, and foreigners.)

7. Genesis 47:28–31: What oath did Jacob ask of Joseph?

8. Genesis 50:22–26: What was Joseph's request?

   What was Joseph's age at his death?

9. Exodus 4:5: Why did the people need to be "convinced"?

10. When Israel was not delivered at the end of four hundred years, what do you think this did to their faith in God?

11. Exodus 1:8–14: Based upon the Scripture, how long were the Israelites slaves? No actual figure is given, so estimate the time.

12. Exodus 1:11–14: What was the impact of this treatment on Israel's ability to govern themselves and to worship God as they had been taught by Jacob?

13. Genesis 47:15–27: What factors might have brought on such contempt toward the Israelites?

    Contrast the Egyptians' situation, who lost their land and sold themselves to Pharaoh, as compared with that of the Israelites, who lived in the best part of Egypt.

God's Call to Moses and Israel

Exodus 2–4; Hebrews 11:23–27: Review Moses' background.

1. What was Moses' temperament and level of self-confidence before he left Egypt?

2. What was his temperament and self-confidence later when God called him?

3. How well does Moses demonstrate faith in God?

   What is God's reaction?

4. How can this be applied in your life?

God Liberates Israel

Exodus 5–15:

1. Exodus 5:2–19: When Moses displays God's power, does Pharaoh respond with respect?

2. Exodus 5:20–23: How strong was Moses' faith here?

    What would you have done?

    How can you apply this to your life?

3. Exodus 7:5: Was God's focus only on liberating Israel?

4. Exodus 5:2; 8:8; 8:25–28; 9:27–28; 10:16–18; 10:24: Record the change in Pharaoh's attitude toward God with each subsequent plague.

    1.
    2.
    3.
    4.
    5.
    6.
    7.
    8.
    9.
    10.

Pharaoh asks Moses to intercede on his behalf. What application can this have in your life?

5. Exodus 14:1–4: Was Pharaoh's decision to pursue the Israelites a surprise?

    If you had been present, how would you have reacted?

    What's the lesson to be learned?

6. Revelation 15:3–4 refers to the song of Moses, which is recorded

in Exodus 15:1–22. What personal experiences would you include in the song of your own journey?

Do you have a song or a Psalm of thanksgiving? If so, write down some of the words below. If not, choose a song that you can sing as a thankful response to what God has done for you.

My personal Song of Thanksgiving is:

7.   Read Psalm 145:14–21, where David reflects on God's faithfulness. How does this relate to His dealings with Israel?

Section 2: Deuteronomy Chapters 1–3

Insights into God's Character

God's generosity

1. Deuteronomy 1:8–11: Moses looked back on the history of Israel, but also painted his dream for their future. What was his dream?

2. 2 Kings 13:17–19: Do you dream? Do you expect great things of God? Do you believe He is generous? Have you ever even thought about it?

   My dream for the future:

3. Deuteronomy 2:7: Did Israel believe they had "gone short of nothing"?

   Does "going short of nothing" mean that you get everything that you want?

   Does this mean you shouldn't ask?

   Read Numbers 11:4–6, Matthew 6:8, 24–34, Hebrews 13:5, and 1 Corinthians 10:9, 10: What's the point God's making?

   Compare this with Philippians 4:6 and 1 Thessalonians 5:16-18. What changes do you need to make?

God's faithfulness

1. Deuteronomy 1:8: God did just as He promised. Does it matter that Abraham, Isaac, and Jacob weren't there to see the promise come true?

187

2. Before Isaac died, he witnessed Joseph's disappearance. Witnessing this tragedy, what do you think Isaac's final thoughts about God's faithfulness were just before he died?

3. Deuteronomy 1:21: God has a track record of faithfulness. Like Israel, we also require little steps before we're able to take big steps. With the many examples in Scripture, should it be easier for us to trust His faithfulness?

   Why or why not?

God's tenderness

1. Deuteronomy 1:31–33: What metaphor is used to show how God helped Israel?

   Is it difficult for you to imagine yourself in this scene? Draw a picture illustrating God carrying you.

God is consistent and fair

Leviticus 18:24; 20:23; Deuteronomy 18:12; Matthew 3:9:

1. Deuteronomy 2:8–13,16–20: What do these verses tell us about our heavenly Father?

2. Deuteronomy 9:5: God said it was not because of Israel's merit that they were being given the land. How then should we view our natural gifts?

   Contrast the difference between the actions you take when you have a thankful spirit compared with those you take with a spirit of obligation.

   How do I feel when I do something because I'm thankful?

   How do I feel when I do something because I have to?

God encourages and inspires

1. Deuteronomy 1:29–30: What does God promise to do here?

Visualize God doing the same for you. What does that picture look like?

Read John 7:37–38; John 14:1, 27; and 15:1-7 to complete the picture.

2. Deuteronomy 3:22: Why shouldn't they be afraid?

   How were they to be sure of victory?

   What is it that makes faith so difficult?

3. Deuteronomy 3:28: "Support and strengthen him, for he will lead this people." Also read Joshua 1:5–9; Isaiah 40:28–31; Mark 14:32-41; and Ephesians 6:19. Why do you think God asks Moses to encourage Joshua?

   What's the lesson for us?

God guides, provides, heals, and protects

1. Deuteronomy 1:42: What happened to God's protection when Israel did not accept His counsel?

2. Deuteronomy 3:1–11: Who won this battle?

   Was there any room for pride in this accomplishment?

   How does this apply to you?

God rewards

1. Deuteronomy 1:36: What did Caleb do that caused the Lord to call him "loyal" and to honor him and his descendants?

2. How was Caleb's faith linked to what he said and did? Read Numbers 13:30–33.

   Who was being realistic, Caleb or his colleagues?

   By believing that faith must be realistic, do you tie God's hands? How?

Read Nehemiah 1. What did Nehemiah do when God opened the door?

God's anger and/or punishment

1. Deuteronomy 1:34: This text refers to Numbers 13–14 when the 12 spies surveyed Canaan. Why was God angry?

2. Deuteronomy 1:37: This text refers to Numbers 20:2–13 when Moses did not uphold God's holiness. Why was God angry here? Also read Psalm 106:32–33.

3. Deuteronomy 2:14–16: There was a penalty for distrust and disobedience. What impact does distrust and fear have on our lives?

   What will you do to correct this problem?

4. Deuteronomy 2:24–30: God impacts events. Do you expect Him to act in your life?

   How can you shift your expectations?

5. Deuteronomy 3:26: "Because of you the Lord angrily brushed me aside and would not listen." Moses still appeared to be blind to his error. Since we know that God resurrected Moses, was this punishment harsh?

   Was the punishment for the benefit of Moses, Israel or both?

   What does this demonstrate about God's mercy?

Our Sinful Character

Fearful, Critical Spirit

1. Deuteronomy 1:26: This text references the story in Numbers 13–14. Why wasn't the fearful spirit of the ten spies justified?

2. Deuteronomy 3:22: Is there a place for fear in your life?

Read Romans 8:14–15; Psalm 34:1–5.

Doubting and Disobedient

1. Deuteronomy 1:21, 26–28: At best, Israel doubted God's ability to fulfill His promise. Even with proof, they muttered treason against God. Do you do this?

   What areas of your life are hardest for you to trust God with?

2. Deuteronomy 1:32–34: Why did they persist in doubting?

   How can you view life's obstacles as opportunities for God to display His power?

Witnesses to God's faithfulness

1. Deuteronomy 3:24: After all Moses saw God do, what's your reaction to his statement?

2. Ephesians 6:9 says God has no favorites and Deuteronomy 10:17 says He is no respecter of persons. What are the implications regarding what we should expect of God in our lives?

Section 3: Deuteronomy 4–5

Exodus 19:5–6: "If only you will now listen to me and keep my covenant, then out of all peoples you will become my special possession; for the whole earth is mine. You will be to me a **kingdom of priests, my holy nation**" (emphasis supplied). This was the covenant God made with Israel.

Revelation 20:6: "Blessed and holy are those who share in this first resurrection! Over them the second death has no power; but **they shall be priests of God** and of Christ, and shall reign with him for the thousand years" (emphasis supplied).

1 Peter 2:9: "But you are a chosen race, a royal priesthood, a dedicated nation, a people claimed by God for his own, to proclaim the glorious deeds of him who has called you out of darkness into his marvellous light."

1. What are the similarities between God's promises to us and the covenant He made with Israel?

2. What does this tell you about God and how He views you?

Insights into God's Character

God's generosity

1. Deuteronomy 4:23; 5:2-3: God made a covenant with Israel that He didn't make with their forefathers. What was the old covenant? Refer to Genesis 28:13.

The covenant given to Abraham, Isaac, and Jacob was about to be fulfilled. This new covenant was more encompassing. It was not limited to Israelites. As you read this new covenant, what's the problem with it?

Read Isaiah 59:21; Jeremiah 31:31-37. God was restoring the original covenant and adding a new element. What was the new element, and why was it added?

2. God made covenants with other people. What were these covenants?

    a. Phineas: Numbers 25:6–13; Psalm 106:28–31

    b. David: 1 Chronicles 17:8–14

    c. Solomon: 2 Chronicles 1:11–12

    d. Jeroboam: 1 Kings 11:37–38

    e. Daniel, Hananiah, Mishael, and Azariah: Daniel 1:8–20

What does this tell you about God's character?

What can it mean for your life?

What does it mean regarding how you pray and bring glory to God's name?

God's faithfulness

1. Deuteronomy 5:10: "But I keep faith with thousands, those who love me and keep my commandments." What is the similar language Jesus used in John 12:50; 14:23; and 15:10?

    Are there commands that everyone should keep and commands that are unique to our own life's journey? Refer to Genesis 12:1; Psalm 25; Isaiah 30:15, 18–21.

God's jealousy

1. In Deuteronomy 5:6–8, God identified who He was and what

He had done. He was to be first in the lives of His people. What authority does God claim in your life?

2. Why was it important to God that they made no carved images or likenesses of anything on the earth or in the waters? Read Exodus 32:1–6, 25.

   They believed their access to God was dependent upon having something visual to represent Him. How does having something visual to represent God affect our faith? Does this limit God?

   Read the story of what it took for Thomas to believe that Jesus had been resurrected in John 20:24–29. How does this apply to your life?

   Imagine you were Thomas. Write down what you would say to Jesus when you saw Him.

3. Deuteronomy 5:11: Why does the wrong use of the Lord's name matter? Read John 16:23–24; Mark 11:22–24.

   1 Corinthians 4:20 says, "For the kingdom of God is not a matter of words, but of power." When God's name is used, should we expect an answer?

   What impact can the wrong use of God's name have on our faith?

God's mercy

1. Deuteronomy 4:41-43: God made provision for the person who killed when overcome with rage. What was this person to do? For a complete picture, read Numbers 35:22–29. Also read Matthew 5:22 and Psalm 103:10.

God guides, provides, heals, and protects

1. Deuteronomy 4:1: What was the purpose of the statutes and laws?

   Is there any mention of salvation in connection to keeping the laws?

Why do you think this is?

2. Deuteronomy 4:6–8: What would be the impact on the surrounding nations? Also read Jeremiah 4:2

3. Consider the following examples of this principle:

Text	Group of People Influenced	What they Learned About God
2 Chronicles 9:1–9		
Daniel 1:12-20		
Daniel 3		
2 Chronicles 17:1–11		

4. Deuteronomy 4:9-14: What were the Israelites called to remember and to share with their children? Refer to Psalms 25, 78, 105, and 106.

   How can you apply these texts?

5. Deuteronomy 4:20–24: Who was Israel to worship?

6. Deuteronomy 4:39–40: Summarize the promise God made to Israel through Moses.

   This is the first instance of the Deuteronomy Promise that Moses repeated twenty times in the book of Deuteronomy. Deuteronomy 5:29 and 5:32–33 give two more examples.

7. Deuteronomy 5:12–15 is the fourth commandment.

   a. Compare with Exodus 20:8–11. What are the differences in the two versions?

      How is God identified in Exodus?

      In Deuteronomy?

   b. The fourth commandment says we are to "remember." Why is this important?

   c. What should we remember?

Hebrews 4:3–11:

Numbers 14:11–23 (background to Hebrews 4:3–11):

Romans 8:12–16:

Psalm 78:4–8:

    d.   Compare Judges 2:10–12 to Psalm 22:22–23; also read Mark 2:27–28. What three things can you do to experience the blessing of the Sabbath?

        1.

        2.

        3.

8.   Deuteronomy 5:16: What is the promise given for honoring our parents?

How does it compare to the promises in Deut. 5:29, 32–33?
What insight does this give us into God's character?
What impact should this have on our willingness to take God at His word?

God rewards

1.   Deuteronomy 4:29–31: What will you find if you seek it?

How must you seek for it?

Jeremiah 31:18-20: How does God feel about Ephraim?

Jeremiah 33:6-9: How does God feel about Judah?

Hosea 11:7-9; 14:1, 2, 4, 5: How does God feel about Israel?

How does God feel about us?

God's anger and/or punishment

1.   Deuteronomy 4:21: Why does Moses tell Israel that God is angry with him?

2. Deuteronomy 4:24, 5:22; 9:18–20; Hebrews 10:26–31: What is the picture of God given here?

    What's the lesson Moses is trying to share from his own experience?

    What impact has fear had on Moses' relationship with God?

    Can a healthy awe/fear of God encourage us to do the right thing and draw us closer to Him?

3. Deuteronomy 4:25-27: What will happen if Israel disobeys God?

    Is God angry? Why or why not?

    What do you learn about God's anger in the following verses?

    a. Zechariah 7:12; 8:2

    b. Jeremiah 6:10; 9:7–9

    c. 2 Kings 13:23

    d. 2 Kings 17 (Note verses 24-27)

    e. Ezekiel 23:28–39 (Note verse 37)

Our Sinful Character

Fearful, Critical Spirit

1. Deuteronomy 5:23-31: How can the fear of God work to our benefit?

    Is God displaying His power as a way to protect the people from themselves?

    What application should this have for each of us? Read Psalm 4:4; 30:5, 10–11.

Misplaced Self-Confidence

1. Deuteronomy 5:25–27 and Exodus 24:3,7,8: How did Israel respond to being in God's presence and hearing His voice?

2. Does their response and subsequent reaction remind you of what frequently happens to your New Year's resolutions?

3. Compare their response with Paul's counsel in Ephesians 6:10–12.

4. Deuteronomy 30:6, 11–14: Where is the word of God?

Section 4: Deuteronomy 6–7

Insights into God's Character

God's generosity

1. Deuteronomy 6 and 7 include three more examples of the Deuteronomy Promise. Summarize each one.

    a. Deuteronomy 6:2–3:

    b. Deuteronomy 6:18, 24:

    c. Deuteronomy 7:12–15:

    What excites you about Deuteronomy 7:13–15?

    What does it tell you about our heavenly Father? Compare this with Matthew 6:25–34.

    What impact can this have on your prayer life?

1. What blessings did Jesus add to this promise?

    a. Matthew 5:17–19:

    b. Matthew 6:27–34:

    c. Matthew 11:28–29:

    d. Mark 8:17–21:

    e. Mark 10:29–31:

God's love and faithfulness

1. Deuteronomy 6:10–12: God will not only do as He promised

Abraham, Isaac, and Jacob, He will do more than they expected. How did Paul express this in 2 Corinthians 2:9 and Ephesians 1:3, 8, 18–19?

2. Deuteronomy 7:9; 1 Chronicles 16:15: For how many generations does God keeps faith?

    How long is a thousand generations? Do the math:
    Average length of a generation: _____ years
    X1000 generations

    =_____years total

    Deuteronomy 10:17–19 and 29:14: Is the one thousand generations long enough to include you?

    Does God intend these promises for you?

    Reflect: So far, is there anything that God has promised that you find distasteful?

God is consistent and fair

1. Deuteronomy 7:7–8: These verses left Israel no room to be proud. Instead, God was faithful to the promise He made to Abraham, Isaac, and Jacob.

God encourages and inspires

1. Deuteronomy 7:6: What is God's vision?

    Is he speaking of the future or the present?

    Compare this with Ephesians 5:1; 1 John 1:7; and 1 John 2:6. What are your conclusions?

God guides, provides, heals, and protects

1. Record the question and answer found in Deuteronomy 6:20, 24.

Question:

Answer:

God's anger and/or punishment

1. Deuteronomy 6:13–15 and 7:4: What did Moses command Israel to do?

    Why was God jealous?

    Why are we to fear Him?

2. Deuteronomy 9:18–20: What did Moses do on behalf of the people and Aaron?

    What happened when Israel forgot that God was dwelling with them? As an example, read Exodus 17:7.

    Why do you think the people turned to idol worship when they had problems?

    Exodus 14:1–4; 10–14: For what purpose did God allow trials to come to them?

    Apply this to your own life.

    God allows problems to happen to me so that:

3. Deuteronomy 7:10, 26: What was the warning about idol worship?

Our Sinful Character

Doubting, Forgetful, and Disobedient

1. Deuteronomy 6:7–9: What were they to do to remember the law?

    a.

    b.

    c.

2. How can you modernize these actions into something appropriate for today?

    a.

    b.

    c.

    Pick one of these actions and make a commitment to do this every day. Write your commitment on sticky note and put it on your mirror, your computer, or in your car to remind yourself.

3. Deuteronomy 7:17–23: How did God accomplish the task of settling Israel into the Promised Land?

4. 2 Chronicles 20:13–30. What did God do to win the battle in this story?

    What part did Israel's army play?

    What is the lesson and its application for us as we face our own battles?

Section 5: Deuteronomy 8–9

Insights into God's Character

God's generosity

1. Read Deuteronomy 8:7–8: What did the land God promised them look like?

    What did this say about God's focus?

    Read Psalm 34:11–19; Psalm 68:5–10; and Jeremiah 17:7–8. What is the central message of these texts?

2. Deuteronomy 8:9: What would Israel never suffer?

3. Psalm 55:22: "Commit your fortunes to the Lord, and he will sustain you; he will never let the righteous be shaken." Also read Psalm 56:3–4,10–11. How focused are you on following God's counsel?

    God promises that His counsel is for your good and that, if you follow it with all your heart, you will be blessed. What impact could a failure to believe this have on your life?

    Reflect: Is this the reason why most of us can't point out the wonderful things He is doing in our lives?

    What does this say about Satan's objectives?

    Does it make it easier to see the mischief he creates in the church?

God is consistent and fair

1. Deuteronomy 9:4–29: How does Moses deal with the temptation of ethnic pride?

    What are the implications for us?

    What's an appropriate attitude?

    How should we treat others?

    Read Luke 9:51–56 and Luke 14:10–24. Can you think of other examples in Scripture in which God encourages reaching out in a spirit of generosity?

God guides, provides, heals, and protects

1. Deuteronomy 8:1: What promise is repeated?

2. Deuteronomy 8:2: What should you remember when you are faced with problems?

    Are you following God for the right motives?

3. Deuteronomy 8:3; Matthew 4:4: Israel was afflicted with hunger. What did this hunger teach them?

    What else did God want them to learn? Read Matthew 7:7–8; 1 Corinthians 10:9–10.

4. Deuteronomy 8:4: Why didn't their clothes wear out or their feet blister for forty years?

    What was the lesson God was teaching them?

5. Have you ever looked at God's commandments as beautiful promises to be embraced?

    How does this change your view of God?

    Does it make it easier to trust God?

Read Psalm 51:6; Hebrews 12:5–12: summarize how God disciplines those He loves.

6. Moses repeated in Deuteronomy 8:16 that it was God's objective to humble them and provide for them in ways they had never known so He might make them prosper. Can you think of an experience where God provided for you in a way you could never have imagined?

If you have had this experience, share the story this week with someone who needs encouragement.

7. Deuteronomy 9:1–3: What was the coming challenge that Moses painted for them?

What was God planning to do for them?

What can you expect God to do about the challenges in your life?

God's anger and/or punishment

1. Deuteronomy 8:19–20: What was the outcome of disobedience?

Do you think God will be easier or harder on those to whom He has given special blessings? Why?

Our Sinful Character

Disobedient, Forgetful, and Proud

1. Deuteronomy 8:11–14: What was the result of forgetting God?

Can you think of times when you've done this?

How does this relate to the purpose of the fourth commandment? (Deuteronomy 5:15 and Exodus 20:11).

2. Deuteronomy 8:15–16: What's the solution to this problem?

3.   What would happen if they forgot (verses 19–20)? Also read Judges 2:10.

Have you ever forgotten what God has done in your life? What happened?

4.   Deuteronomy 9:4: Moses predicted that Israel would believe they deserved God's blessings because they were superior to the other nations. Do you see this same spirit in the church today?

5.   Deuteronomy 9:22 refers to Taberah and Massah. Read the background in Numbers 11:1–3 and Exodus 17:1–7.

   a.   What were they complaining about?

   Were their complaints reasonable? What should they have done instead?

   What would you have done?

   Read Psalm 78 again. Also read Psalm 106. How does this apply to us?

   b.   Deuteronomy 9:27: What did God equate distrust with?

   Numbers 14:23: How many times did they challenge God?

6.   Moses acted as an intercessor for Israel in Deuteronomy 10:26–29 and Numbers 14:10–23. Was this a special and unique role, or is this a role we, too, are called to fill?

Summarize the following texts:

   a.   John 17:18:

   b.   John 20:20-23:

   c.   1 Samuel 12:23–25:

   d.   Daniel 9:15–20:

   e.   Nehemiah 1:5–11:

What impact will this have on your prayer experience?

Read 1 John 3:21–22. What does this demonstrate regarding God's character?

Section 6: Deuteronomy 10–11

In Chapter 10, Moses continues his historical review. In Chapter 11, he once again repeats the Deuteronomy Promise, its conditions, and the results of disobedience.

1. Deuteronomy 10:1–5 reviews how God wrote a second tablet of the Ten Commandments after Moses broke the first set. For the complete story, read Exodus 32–34.

    a. Exodus 32:25: What kind of behavior did Moses observe?

        To see a similar situation, read the story of Balaam in Numbers 24–25.

        In Numbers 25:12, what covenant did God make with Phinehas, son of Eleazar and grandson of Aaron, in response to his commitment?

    b. Exodus 32:28–29; Deuteronomy 10:8–9: Why did God choose the Levites to be priests?

        Was this what God originally intended? Read Exodus 19:5–6.

        Exodus 32:30: What was Moses' tone when he spoke to the people?

        If you were in the crowd when Moses spoke, how would you have felt?

        Leviticus 19:17–18: How would you feel if someone you respected corrected you? How would you respond?

    c. The house of Aaron was also given a special position/role because of the other Levites' sin. Read Numbers 16–17. Why would God offer any of these promises if He knew they would break the covenant?

What does His willingness to make the offer tell us about His character? Does it demonstrate God's tremendous love?

He continually offers warnings and promises to encourage and inspire us. What impact does this have on how you make personal choices?

What does this mean for you when making a life-changing decision? Does it build your confidence to know that, by faith, you can be successful?

2. Deuteronomy 10:6–9: Who died and who succeeded him?

    For the complete story, read Numbers 20:6–29.

    What does God mean in verse 12?

    Is He being unreasonable? Explain.

    Where does the transforming power of grace fit in?

3. Deuteronomy 10:10–11: Of what did Moses remind the people?

    Read Exodus 32:30–33:23 and Exodus 34:27–35. Describe what Moses looked like after he was in God's presence.

    How do you think the people acted when they saw him?

    How would you have felt if you had been there?

Insights into God's Character

God's tenderness and love

1. Deuteronomy 10:14–15: Moses emphasized God's special love for their forefathers. He hadn't forgotten them. What did that say regarding His love for those who placed their faith in Him?

2. Deuteronomy 10:15–17: Because God demonstrated His commitment to them, what were the people to do? The special relationship God had with Abraham, Isaac, and Jacob was open to them too!

God is consistent and fair

1. Deuteronomy 10:17–19: Whom are we called to **love?**

2. Also read Exodus 12:48–49; 1 Kings 8:41–43. Review how Jesus treated foreigners in John 4:1–42; Luke 4:4:25–28; Luke 17:11–19; Ephesians 6:9. This gives us confidence that God's promises are also ours to claim. This is the basis of the confidence John expresses in 1 John 3:21–22.

3. What are the implications of these verses?

4. What actions can you take?

God encourages and inspires

1. Deuteronomy 10:21–22: Whose problem is it if you don't have anything for which to praise God?

   What steps do you need to take to make sure you have something to boast about?

2. Deuteronomy 11:1–7: How do you love the Lord your God?

   Why should you love the Lord your God?

   What personal stories do you have?

   Like the Israelite children, if you don't have your own story, what should you do?

God guides, provides, heals, and protects

1. Moses repeated the Deuteronomy Promise four more times in

Deuteronomy 10:13; 11:8–9; 11:13–15; and 11:18–19. What is the promise again, and what do you think is the purpose of all this repetition?

2. Deuteronomy 11:10–13: Moses once again shared what a wonderful land they were about to enter. Why did he keep repeating this? What was he trying to do?

God rewards

1. Deuteronomy 11:22–25: What was Israel assured about?

God's anger and/or punishment

1. Deuteronomy 11:16–17, 26–27, 32–33: What was the warning Moses gave them?

Section 7: Deuteronomy 12–14

Before reading the laws Moses gave, reread Deuteronomy 4:1–8. What did he say was the purpose of these decrees? Remember, there was no legislative branch in Israel to pass regulations. As you read, it's important to remember that the directions God gave Moses were the law of the land.

Read Psalm 119, the longest chapter of the Bible. What impact was the law supposed to have on us:

    a.   *Personally?*

    b.   *Corporately?*

Insights into God's Character

God's generosity

1. Deuteronomy 14:22–23: What actions were Israel asked to take?

    What was the result of completing these actions?

    In verses 24–26, what are you to do when God blesses you?

2. If you could design an annual celebration to rejoice over the blessings God has provided, what would it look like? Who would you invite? What kind of activities would be involved? What would you eat? What would you wear? What kind of music would you play? Describe your celebration here:

    What is stopping you from doing this?

3. In Deuteronomy 14:29, God promised to bless Israel in everything they did. As with all of His promises, there was a condition in verses 27–28. See also Deuteronomy 26:12; Proverbs 19:17; Proverbs 28:27. What was the condition?

4. How well did Israel follow this command? Refer to Ezekiel 16:48–49; Luke 7:21–23; 14:12–14.

   What's the good news that Jesus brought to the poor?

   Is it possible to follow this counsel with heart felt joy rather than to share out of obligation? How?

   Personal steps I can take to share with joy:

   a.

   b.

   c.

   Things my church can do to share with joy:

   a.

   b.

   c.

God guides, provides, heals, and protects

1. The Deuteronomy Promise is repeated yet again in Deuteronomy 12:28.

2. Deuteronomy 14:1–2: Of what did God remind Israel before moving into the next set of instructions?

3. Deuteronomy 14:3–21: What were some of the health principles that Moses gave the people?

   a.

   b.

c.

d.

Why was this counsel given to them?

Why should we be concerned with health principles today?

What one change can you make today that will improve your health?

Today I will _____
to become more healthy.

God rewards

1. Deuteronomy 12:5–7; 12:11–18; 14:26: What was the reward to those who came to worship the Lord at the place of His choosing?

    What was it that caused them to find joy?

    Was it simply because they went through the motions of bringing a sacrifice? Explain.

    Read Isaiah 1:11–16 and Amos 5:21–24. What had Israel's worship turned into?

    Read Paul's description of the sacrificial system in Hebrews 10. What was the sacrificial system a symbol of?

    Adam and Abraham presented sacrifices. What made their offerings an act of faith?

2. Deuteronomy 14:29: What is the promise?

God's anger and/or punishment

1. Deuteronomy 13:5, 11–16: For what was the death sentence given?

    What was the reason for such a harsh sentence (see verse 11)?

2. Jeremiah 19:5; Leviticus 18:21; 20:2; Jeremiah 9:2, 7, 9. Identify

some of the rites involved in worshiping other gods and what effect these rites had on the character of the worshippers.

Does this make you angry?

How do you think God feels?

Are there similar things that happen in our world today that you can help to change?

3. Deuteronomy 13:17–19: Was God's fierce anger appropriate?

If God is omnipresent—everywhere—does a visual representation of Him limit our idea of who He is?

Remember Thomas? Read John 20:29. What should our faith in God rest on?

Our Sinful Character

Doubting and Disobedient

1. Deuteronomy 12:2–4 and 29–32: What were they commanded to do?

What was the purpose of this command?

What did the kings generally do?

> 2 Chronicles 20:32–33:

> 1King 12:25–33:

2. Read Deuteronomy 12:8; Judges 17:6; 21:25; Genesis 3:5. Read the horrific story in Judges 19–21: What's the common thread?

Can you think of any other examples?

What's the lesson?

Is it safe to decide for yourself what is right or wrong? Explain.

Section 8: Deuteronomy 15–16

Insights into God's Character

God's generosity

1. Deuteronomy 15:4–5: What promise did Moses repeat?

2. Verses 7–8: What counsel did Moses give regarding the poor?

   Read Luke 7:22. What was the good news that Jesus brought to the poor?

   Summarize the advice found in 2 Corinthians 9:6–14:

1. Verses 9–11: What is the theme of these verses?

   How does the message in these verses relate to the following texts?

   a. Deuteronomy 8:16–18:

   b. Deuteronomy 10:19–22:

   c. Proverbs 11:23–26:

   d. Proverbs 14:21, 31 :

   e. Proverbs 19:16–17:

   f. Ezekiel 16:48–50:

2. Read Proverbs 18:4; 20:4; 15:19: How are we to respond to those who refuse to work?

   What about someone who has made mistakes in the past?

What should we do when we help and get burned?

What do the following promises tell us about the outcomes we desire?

    a.   Psalm 41:1:

    b.   Psalm 112:1, 9:

3.   Deuteronomy 15:12–17: How did God say slaves should be treated?

4.   Deuteronomy 15:19–22: What part of their flocks were the Israelites to give?

How can this be applied to your tithes and offerings?

When Moses writes that we are to eat in the presence of the Lord, what visual picture comes to mind?

God guides, provides, heals, and protects

1.   Deuteronomy 16:1–8: What was this festival and what historical event was it celebrating?

What was the significance of this festival relative to Jesus' life and death?

2.   Deuteronomy 16:9–12: What is this festival called?

This is the anniversary of when God gave the law at Mt. Sinai.

1 Corinthians 15:20: What is the Messianic application? See also Romans 8:23 and James 1:18.

3.   Deuteronomy 16:13–17: What is the name of this festival?

Leviticus 23:41–44: What is the historical background for the festival?

How do you think the theme of this festival can apply to your experience today?

What impact were these vacation days to have on Israel's faith in God?

What impact would they have on maintaining a spirit of joy, humility, gratitude, and generosity? Read 2 Chronicles 29–31:

What is the mood in Deuteronomy 16:11, 14–15, 17?

Imagine that you lived in a place and time that celebrated the Jewish festivals. How would you feel about them? Would you look forward to them or think that they were a chore?

What do you think was God's purpose in setting up a yearly cycle of festivals?

4. Deuteronomy 16:18–20: What is the theme of this section?

Section 9: Deuteronomy 17–19

Insights into God's Character

God's anger and/or punishment

1. Deuteronomy 17: What is the listed order of the violations of God's law?

   Do you think this is in order of importance? Why or why not?

2. Deuteronomy 17:7, 12–13; 19:19–20; 22:21–22, 24;24:7: What repeated phrase or similar language did God use regarding punishment?

   If the punishment was administered as God directed, how often would Israel have had to deal with these problems?

   What was the accompanying promise?

   What would have been the biggest challenge the people would have faced?

   What lesson can you apply to your own life from this method?

God guides, provides, heals, and protects

1. Deuteronomy 18:9–14: What did God prohibit Israel from doing?

2. Deuteronomy 18:15–22. What were the guidelines for testing a prophet?

   How did Amos 3:7 make this clear?

What did Jeremiah add? (Jeremiah 28:1–9).

God rewards

Deuteronomy 18:1–8: Why was reward and honor given to the Levites?

God's mercy

1. Deuteronomy 19:1–9: What were the guidelines for the cities of refuge?

   Read Matthew 5:21–22. How did Jesus raise the standard?

   What does Romans 12:17–21 add?

2. Deuteronomy 19:10–13 and 19–21: How did this process ensure that no innocent blood would be shed?

   What was the promise (verse 13) that accompanied this command?

   What was the principle Jesus taught in Matthew 5:38–48 and Matthew 19:8?

   Would the same principle work today in your city? Why or why not?

3. Psalm 119:152, 160, 165: What are the benefits of a life based on God's instruction?

Our Sinful Character

Greed

1. Deuteronomy 17:16–17: What were the instructions given to Israel's future kings regarding the acquiring of wealth and wives?

What was the warning in 2 Chronicles 7:19–22?

What was the punishment listed in 1 Kings 11:4–13?

2. How might we apply Deuteronomy 17:20?

What's the key principle?

Section 10: Deuteronomy 20–25

Insights into God's Character

God's tenderness

1. Deuteronomy 20:7 and 24:5: What did a newly married man NOT have to do? Also read Proverbs 5:18.

2. Deuteronomy 22:1–4: What is the emphasis in these verses?

3. Deuteronomy 22:6–7 To what is this promise of prosperity and long life tied?

    Does this surprise you?

    How else might this be applied?

4. Deuteronomy 24:10–15: What guidelines are given here?

5. Deuteronomy 25:1–3: What is the purpose of punishment?

God is consistent and fair

In Deuteronomy 25:13–16, God stresses the importance of integrity in all of our dealings with each other. Read Psalm 25:21; Proverbs 11:1–3; and Proverbs 13:6. What does this mean?

God encourages and inspires

1. Deuteronomy 20:1–4, 8: Before every battle, Israel is commanded

to have no fear when facing formidable odds and to go forward with confidence. What were they to remember?

If they continued to be afraid, what happened to them?

What does this tell you about the deceptiveness of negative appearances?

What will you do when faced with horrible obstacles?

Compare this language to Ephesians 6:10–18.

2. Deuteronomy 20:5–7: Who was not supposed to go into battle?

What do you think was the purpose for these exemptions?

Did these exemptions increase the probability that those in battle were focused and determined?

God guides, provides, heals, and protects

1. Deuteronomy 20:16–18: What land was Israel limited to conquering?

Why do you think this was so?

2. Deuteronomy 21:15–17: Whom was God showing protection towards?

3. In Deuteronomy 25:5–7: Who were provisions made for?

God's anger and/or punishment

1. Deuteronomy 22:13–30: What is the theme of this passage?

What similar language do you find in verses 21, 22, and 24?

2. Deuteronomy 22:28–29; 24:1–4: What was Moses' counsel regarding divorce?

Malachi 2:13–16: Compare these verses with Moses' counsel.

Matthew 19:6–9: What did Jesus say?

Since many of the same problems have continued throughout history, do you think the counsel is still relevant? Explain.

If God were to speak to us at Mt. Sinai today, what counsel do you think He would give us regarding marriage?

3. Deuteronomy 23:3–6: What group was forbidden to worship with Israel?

    How long did this prohibition last?

    Read Genesis 19:30–38: Who were they descended from?

    Review the following references for additional background and insight.

    a. Judges 3:14, 30: Who rules whom, and for how long?

    b. Judges 10: Who harasses Israel for eighteen years?

    c. 2 Kings 23:10; 16:3; 21:6: How did the Ammonites worship?

        What did King Solomon's Ammonite wives lead him to do?

    d. Isaiah 15–16; Jeremiah 48–49: What will happen to these groups?

        Why do you think God placed such a strong prohibition against intermarriage between Israel and these other groups?

        What was He trying to achieve?

    e. Ruth 1–4: Ruth was a Moabite woman who was only three generations removed from the prohibition against intermarriage. Why do you think God blesses Ruth and Boaz's marriage and allows King David and Jesus to descend from their line?

4. Deuteronomy 21:18–21: What measures were outlined for the correction of extremely rebellious children?

    Do you notice any familiar language in Verse 21?

Section 11: Deuteronomy 26–30

Insights into God's Character

God's generosity

1. Deuteronomy 26 focuses on what Israel was to do when they experienced the promised blessings. Why did Moses need to tell them what to say and when to say it?

   How might we apply this same principle?

2. In Deuteronomy 29:47, what was the one issue that would bring curses on Israel?

   Why do you think this was so important?

3. Deuteronomy 26:18–19: This is a repeat of Moses' promise. What is the important new twist?

4. Deuteronomy 28:9–14; 29:9; 30:15, 19–20: Here's the promise again! Can you write it from memory by now?

   Read 1 Corinthians 2:9–10; 2 Corinthians 3:18; Ephesians 1:8, 18. What did Paul desire for the followers of Christ?

5. Deuteronomy 30:16, 20 repeats the Deuteronomy Promise. Do you think it's been repeated often enough? Isn't it amazing that most of us are unfamiliar with this promise?

   Imagine you are asked to explain the Deuteronomy Promise to a fifth grader. How would you put it into words that they could understand?

The Deuteronomy Promise is:

God is consistent and fair

1. We have already seen that the promises extend for a thousand generations (Deuteronomy 7:9). Moses restates this idea again in Deuteronomy 29:14. Do these promises create a positive motivator for you?

   How does this change your view of God?

God encourages and inspires

1. In Deuteronomy 29 Moses reviews Israel's past, provides proof of God's leading, and once again warns them of the terrible outcomes if they reject God. Why do you think he repeats this message?

   Compare Deuteronomy 29:5 with Deuteronomy 8:3–5. What was God trying to communicate?

God guides, provides, heals, and protects

1. Deuteronomy 30 is a chapter of prophetic reassurance that, despite their disobedience, God promises to restore the Israelites, transform their hearts, and make them more prosperous than their forefathers. See verses 5–6, 9–11.

2. Deuteronomy 30:11–14: How difficult of a task did Moses say this was?

God's anger and/or punishment

1. Deuteronomy 28:15–68: Moses outlines the curses for failing to serve God with gladness. Review Exodus 32:25; 2 Chronicles 28:19; Jeremiah 31:18–20, 36–37; Lamentations 3:19–26, 31–33; Ephesians 6:10–12; 1 Peter 5:8; Lamentations 3:33; 1 Peter 5:8.

2. What conclusions do you draw regarding God's role and Satan's role in the curses?

3. What is the application to your life?

Our Sinful Character

Forgetful, Doubting, and Disobedient

1. Deuteronomy 27:1–8: To keep Israel from being forgetful, what were the people to do with the words Moses gave them?

2. Deuteronomy 27:11–26: What were the tribes of Israel to pronounce?

Section 12: Deuteronomy 31–34

Deuteronomy 31: Moses attempts to reassure the people and encourages them to establish traditions to ensure that they remember what God has done and desires to do in their lives.

Deuteronomy 32: Moses recites a song and gives his final warning.

Deuteronomy 33: Moses blesses each tribe of Israel. In verses 28–29, what is the promise given by Moses?

Deuteronomy 34: Moses dies and Israel mourns. What's unique about Moses' death? (Deuteronomy 34:7)

What strikes you about the last three verses of the chapter?

What can we learn from these three verses?

Insights into God's Character

God guides, provides, heals, and protects

1. Deuteronomy 31:5, 8: What is the central message about God's character?

2. Deuteronomy 32:1–14: List three blessings God was prepared to give Israel.

   a.

   b.

c.

3. Deuteronomy 32:47: It's the Deuteronomy Promise one last time!

4. Deuteronomy 33:3–4: What does God give His people because he loves them?

5. Deuteronomy 33:28–29: What was the happy ending described here?

God's anger and/or punishment

1. Deuteronomy 32:19–43: Summarize God's response to Israel's future unfaithfulness.

   Are we any better than Israel?

2. Deuteronomy 32:15-18: What does Moses mean in verse 18?

   How does this apply?

3. Deuteronomy 32:51–52; Jude 9; Matthew 17:3–4: What happens to Moses?

Our Sinful Character

Doubting and Disobedient

1. Deuteronomy 31:6–8: What were the Israelites encouraged to be?

2. Deuteronomy 31:10–13: What were the foreigners to learn from Israel?

3. Deuteronomy 31:14–21: Describe this amazing scene where God comes one last time to talk to Moses.

4. Deuteronomy 31:23: What is Joshua's commission?

5. Deuteronomy 33:15–18: What did God predict Israel would do?

If you had been present, what would you have felt?

Could this serve as a motivator for change?

After reading the counsel given, accompanied by the promises, has your need to experience God's grace in your life increased? Explain.

Does James 2:18–26 bring new meaning to the role of faith and works?

Witnesses to God's faithfulness

1. Deuteronomy 32: This is the song Moses taught Israel. Using your own lyrics or those of an existing song, write your own song of deliverance. Include the lyrics here:

Take it with You

1. What is your favorite part of Deuteronomy?

2. If you were to recommend that someone read a section of Deuteronomy, what section would it be? Why?

3. What is the single most important concept you have learned from Deuteronomy?

4. Deuteronomy in a nutshell: Explain the theme of Deuteronomy.

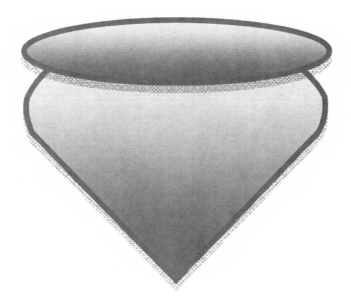

5. Interview three people. Ask them what first comes to mind when they hear the word "Deuteronomy"?

   a.

b.

c.

6. Compare their answers to your view of Deuteronomy:

7. Restate the Deuteronomy Promise:

8. The Deuteronomy Promise says that God wants to bless us if we obey his laws. Choose one promise from the Bible that you would like to claim in your life. Write it here:

9. How has this study changed your view of God and His character?

10. What is your vision of what you would like your relationship with God to be?

11. Do you have any new expectations of God?

   I expect that God will:

12. How will you share your new understanding of God's character with others?

I hope that this study has given you a clearer picture of Jesus and our heavenly Father. His faithfulness will amaze you, humble you, and leave you in awe.

The author would be happy to receive your comments or stories of what this book has meant in your personal experience. He may be contacted at:

dennis@overlookedpromises.com

Or,

Dennis Williams, Jr.
P.O. Box 2038
Ferndale, WA 98248

CPSIA information can be obtained at www.ICGtesting.com
Printed in the USA
BVOW011313230212

283663BV00001B/5/P

9 781462 706174